Scotland's Story
in Her Monuments

Scotland's Story in Her Monuments

by
David Graham-Campbell

Foreword by
Lord Home of the Hirsel, P.C., K.T.

ROBERT HALE · LONDON

Robert Hale Limited
Clerkenwell House
45–47 Clerkenwell Green
London EC1R 0HT

ISBN 0 7091 9543 5

Photoset by Rowland Phototypesetting Ltd
Printed in Great Britain by
St Edmundsbury Press, Bury St Edmunds, Suffolk
and bound by Hunter & Foulis

Wade's Bridge, Aberfeldy, designed by William Adam, 1733. The figure of the soldier is that of one of the mutineers who protested when the Government shabbily marched the regiment south on the pretext that it was to be reviewed by the King (who was not even in the country) but really in order to ship abroad men who had enlisted on the understanding that they were only to be employed at home.

Contents

Illustrations

Foreword

by Lord Home of the Hirsel, P.C., K.T.

It always needs a stretch of the imagination to recognize the personalities of history as being people like us.

In this book Mr Graham-Campbell has pictured the lives of Scottish churchmen and kings, nobles and commoners by taking their monuments and illustrating from them their characters, their lives and their deeds. Saints like Magnus, Ninian and Columba who founded the monasteries; kings like Malcolm and David who enriched Scotland with their palaces and abbeys; and the heads of great families who in war and .peace hit the headlines of the day: Campbell, MacLeod, Douglas, Borthwick, Haig, Barrie, Dunbar, Ross, Kennedy and many more who are still household names and who left their mark on their generation and their castles and their tombs for posterity.

The skill of the workers in stone and metal, whether it be in the great historic crosses of the early Christian days or in the grouping of figures engaged in their warlike or peaceful pursuits, tells us of their looks, their clothes, their habits and the features of the countryside in which they lived.

The author too has been able to mark and to time the changes of form and style from the earliest period, through the traumatic years of the Stewarts to the Reformation and then to the industrialization of central Scotland in the Victorian age.

The whole is an arresting and revealing story and goes a long way to explain our Scottish heritage and the sort of people we are.

Acknowledgements

My first thanks are owing to Lord Home of the Hirsel for his Foreword.

I am also grateful to all those who have given permission to me to reproduce illustrations, and especially grateful to the staff of the Royal Commission on the Ancient and Historical Monuments of Scotland for help on many occasions. The following illustrations are reproduced from their collection: Nos 9, 10, 13, 14, 23, 26, 27a, 27b, 27c, 28, 29, 30, 32, 33, 34, 47, 51, 53, 54, 62, 65, 67, 68, 69, 71, 75, 82, 90.

I should like to express my thanks to the Duke of Argyll for allowing a photograph to be taken in the Argyll Mausoleum at Kilmun (No. 41); to the Duke of Hamilton for the use of the drawing of the third Duke's tomb (No. 67), and to the Earl of Lauderdale for the illustration used on the jacket (and as No. 58). This is Crown Copyright and is reproduced by permission of the Scottish Development Department, as are Nos 1, 2, 3, 5a, 5b, 6a, 8, 11, 12, 15, 18, 21, 24, 25, 31, 39, 56, 58, and 70.

Nos 4 and 6b are by permission of the National Museum of the Antiquities of Scotland; Nos 17, 35, 59, 66 and 83 by Hubert Fenwick; No. 41 by the author; No. 45 by courtesy of the Court of the University of Aberdeen and No. 55 by that of the Earl of Strathmore and the Pilgrim Press.

Nos 48, 50, 63, 72, 74, 76, 80, 84, 85, 86, 91, 93, 95, 99 and the frontispiece are reproduced by permission of the Scottish Tourist Board; Nos 61 and 92 by Color Photo Ltd; No. 64 by Jonathan Gibson and *Country Life*, No. 73 by Glasgow District Council.

Miss Betty Willsher very kindly allowed me to use three illustrations (Nos 76, 78, 79) from Willsher and Hunter, *18th Century Gravestones*, published by Canongate Publishing. The photograph of the Prince Consort's statue, taken by Henry Jolles, is reproduced by gracious permission of Her Majesty the Queen (No. 92).

No. 96 is reproduced by permission of the Trustees of the National War Memorial; No. 97 by Mr McLean Mitchell (Clapperton); No. 98 by Studio Tyrrell; Nos 100 and 101 are by courtesy of Mr Hugh Lorimer and Mrs Paul Shillibear.

The line drawings are taken from MacGibbon and Ross, *Ecclesiastical Architecture of Scotland* and Anderson, *Scotland in Early Christian times*.

The passage on p. 34 is quoted by permission of Robert Hale Ltd from *The Ancient Stones of Scotland* by Dr W. Douglas Simpson, and that on pages 46–9 from *The Medieval Stone-carver in Scotland*, by J. S. Richardson, by permission of The Edinburgh University Press.

I would like to thank Professor Gordon Donaldson for allowing me to read and to quote from an unpublished paper, "Some 16th and 17th Century Monuments"; and Dr Ronald Cant for reading this book in typescript and for his most helpful suggestions. He is in no way responsible for any opinions expressed nor for any errors which remain.

Lastly, and not for the first time, I am indebted to Mr Charles Millar for stimulating criticism, new ideas, and help with reading the proofs.

Preface

The monuments of a country can clothe with flesh, as no written words can, the bare bones of its history, and can convince us that the names in that story once belonged to living men and women. That Scotland lost all too much of her heritage at the time of the Reformation, and by subsequent neglect, is known to everyone; what is less well known is the extent of what has survived.

The prehistoric period—the days before we know the name of any single inhabitant of the lands that make up what we now call Scotland—is exceptionally rich. If we have no cave paintings to rival those of France and Spain, the economy, the precision, and the sheer beauty of the incised slabs of the Picts can bear comparison with any tribal works of art. And, among the structural monuments, the concept of the great stone circle at Callanish, and the close fit of the massive slabs in the tomb at Maeshowe, are no less impressive.

From the next age, when we have names but little more—and history tends to be hagiography—there are the carved cross-slabs of the Picts and some fine Scottish crosses; and the churches of Dunfermline Abbey, Sweetheart Abbey and Kirkwall bear witness to the reality (and also the *pietas*) of King David I and his parents, of Devorguilla of Galloway, and of the Norse Earl Rognvald. All that remains of the alabaster tomb of Robert the Bruce are a few small fragments in the National Museum of Antiquities in Edinburgh, but there is the incised slab of his comrade Sir William Oliphant at Aberdalgie, and the canopy from his daughter Margaret's tomb in Paisley Abbey. Nor are some of the modern memorials to Bruce and to Wallace to be despised.

From the following century, there is the elaborate armoured figure of Margaret's grandson, the Wolf of Badenoch, at Dunkeld—though no man ever deserved less to have a place of honour in a church. And hardly less grand is the armour on the incised slab of Sir Gilbert de Greenlaw who was killed in the important, if now misty, Battle of Harlaw.

The ecclesiastics, for their part, provide some fine effigies. There is a thirteenth-century bishop in the ruined Cathedral of Moray, a Cistercian abbot at Dundrennan, and a fourteenth-century abbot at Iona. Without its effigy but a marvel of intricate carving is the tomb of Bishop Kennedy who founded St Salvator's College at St Andrews and died in 1460.

Many laymen were commemorated by recumbent slabs and in the West Highlands particularly a beautiful tradition of carving was evolved, using foliage, weapons, animals and human figures in low relief. From the fifteenth century some very remarkable wall tombs of laymen have survived and, since by that time the heads of the House of Douglas were often as powerful as the Kings themselves, it is natural that they should be especially well represented. Quite different in style and probably of foreign workmanship is one tomb from another family which was in due course to present a similar threat to the throne—that of Sir Duncan Campbell of Loch Awe, 1453.

In 1513 the defeat at Flodden left its mark deep on the nation's consciousness, not only in such traditions as the annual games at Ceres and the ceremony observed at the Common Riding at Selkirk (and the later "Flowers of the Forest"), but in a contemporary monument to the Lord Sempill killed in that fight. But, in general, the 1500s are less rich because the Reformation discouraged the commemoration of the dead, lest men should be tempted to offer prayers for their souls, and its leaders also forbade burial in church (not always with success). When wall monuments do come into fashion again, there are fewer effigies, and the central recess is often much shallower and contains merely an inscription or a coat of arms; that of the Regent Moray in St Giles is an early example, and is also one of the few surviving Scottish brasses.

It is perhaps not stretching a point too far to include gardens as memorials. The earliest ones date from this time, planted by men for their heirs and, one cannot but feel, so that posterity should remember them. Edzell and Pitmedden have been recently recreated and are now maintained by the Scottish Development Department and the National Trust for Scotland respectively. The lay-out of the former is in honour of the Union of the Crowns in 1603.

With the reign of James VI, wall monuments came into fashion again, mostly of the modified type just described; where effigies exist, the subjects are now usually shown standing or kneeling rather than recumbent. Then the disturbed times of Civil War, and the ethos of the Cromwellian Protectorate, produced another hiatus; the only memorials to Montrose and Argyll are nineteenth-century.

From 1603—and still more from the Union of the Parliaments in 1707—those whose ambition was to gain high office, or to influence policy, had more and more to live their lives in England, and thus were often buried there too. On the whole the most beautiful and the most interesting stones of the eighteenth century are those of the middling class of people which may be found in graveyards throughout the country, though naturally they are most common in the more prosperous Lowlands.

With the Golden Age of art and learning of the late eighteenth century, and the technological advances of the nineteenth, monuments in the form of statues unconnected with burials become common. Unfortunately it was not a time of outstanding sculptors but many of the works are lifelike and have some vigour, and most are of some historical interest. And so to the memorials of our own times, and especially the memorials of the two World Wars.

The purpose of this book is to illustrate the evolution of custom in these matters and, so far as space permits, the richness of our national heritage, and also to place in their historical context the men and events commemorated.

ONE

Scotland up to A.D. 1100

Prehistoric times

Scotland's earliest immigrants were food-gatherers, Mesolithic people who left nothing behind them in the way of monuments; but the Neolithic peasants who followed them built Megalithic tombs, unmistakably monumental. These, which may date from around 2000 B.C., are of two main kinds: first, galleried graves in which a rectangular chamber was covered with a long cairn of stones; and, secondly, passage graves in which the central chamber lay under a round cairn.

The earliest inhabitants also constructed henges, ritual earthworks, surrounded by a ditch and bank, with a circle of wood or stones—clearly ceremonial, less certainly commemorative. There is however at Callanish in the Island of Lewis a great circle of stones which is part of the same complex as a chambered tomb, even if it is not definitely of the same date. Some of the smaller circles certainly have primary burials.

A galleried grave of the type mentioned above may be seen at Cairnholy in Kirkcudbrightshire, four miles south-east of Creetown, overlooking Wigtown Bay. It has a crescent forecourt and a double chamber, and remains have been found there from both Neolithic and Beaker days. It was quite usual for such graves (and for passage graves) to be used more than once.

2. *Callanish Stone Circle, Lewis. This is the finest circle of Megalithic
standing stones in Scotland and may date from about the second millennium* B.C. *There is an avenue of nineteen stones leading to a circle of
thirteen, beyond which the avenue continues briefly; and a cross avenue
provides short transepts. Inside the circle stands a megalith fifteen feet high
and five feet wide and, uncharacteristically, a cairn, now roofless, which
covered a burial. The circle at Callanish measures thirty-seven feet across,
but a henge at Stenness on the mainland of Orkney is a hundred feet across
and lies within a ditch of twice that diameter. More accessible, but smaller,
are circles in Perthshire at Croftmoraig near Taymouth and Monzie,
Crieff, and in Argyll at Temple Wood, Kilmartin.*

3. Maeshowe, Orkney. Under a large round grass-covered mound of clay and stones is a low, stone-lined passage leading to a burial chamber fifteen feet square; off it lie three smaller chambers, all formerly closed with great stone blocks. The stones which make the corbelled roof weigh up to three tons yet fit so well that in places it is difficult to insert even the blade of a penknife between them. The building skills required and the scale of the tomb suggest a high degree of social organization and indeed of subservience to a powerful leader. Unfortunately the mound has been robbed and damaged on more than one occasion—in distant days by Viking expeditions such as that of Earl Rognvald in 1150 who looted what was described as "a great treasure" (perhaps golden articles originating in the Mediterranean lands) and more recently in 1861, when the main structural damage was done. The Norse visitors left inscriptions in their Runic script and also carvings of a lion or dragon, a seal and a serpent knot.

For other examples of these types of monument the reader is referred to: R. Feachem, *Guide to Prehistoric Scotland*; E. W. McKie, *Scotland: An Archaeological Guide*; or for more comprehensive treatment to: A. S. Henshall, *Prehistoric Chambered Tombs of Scotland*.

Further immigrations followed—of people who buried their dead in short stone cists, individually and with a characteristic earthenware vessel, a Beaker; of bronze-using men who cremated their dead and buried them in urn-fields; and of iron-using men building great hill-forts and (in certain areas) brochs. But, striking as their remains are—especially their stone houses at Skara Brae in Orkney and Jarlshof in Shetland, and their brochs—they tend to be utilitarian rather than commemorative.

Roman times

The Romans arrived in the first century A.D. Their interest in Scotland may be likened to that of Britain in Afghanistan during the nineteenth century. They sought to protect their settlements in England rather than to colonize Scotland; there are no large villas or towns. Under Agricola, the forward policy was predominant and Lowland Scotland was invaded from south-west to north-east; but, in the second century, Rome passed to the defensive, building first Hadrian's stone wall, and then its outpost line of defence in turf—the Antonine Wall from Forth to Clyde—in A.D. 142. There was another move forward by Severus in the third century but the fourth saw a steady decline. The chief Roman remains are their military camps, roads, weapons and so on, but there is a tablet, found at Bridgeness near Bo'ness, commemorating the completion of 4652 paces of wall by the Second Legion. This, and a tombstone depicting three legionaries, is in the National Museum of Antiquities in Edinburgh, and there are other Roman carvings in the museums of Glasgow and Dundee.

4. A distance slab from the Antonine Wall. On the left is a Roman cavalryman with four disarmed natives at his mercy; on the right, a Roman purification ceremony. The inscription reads: "IMP[ERATORI] CAES[ARI] TITO AELIO HADRI[ANO] ANTONINO AUG-[USTO] PIO P[ATRI] P[ATRIAE] LEG[IO] II AUG[USTA] PER M[ILIA] P[ASSUUM] IIII DCLII FEC[IT]"—"To the Emperor Caesar Titus Aelius Hadrianus Antoninus Augustus Pius, Father of his Country, the Second Legion, Augusta, made [this] over 4,652 paces." This is the best-known distance slab from the Antonine Wall, A.D. 142, found at Bridgeness, at the eastern end, near Bo'ness in 1868. A replica of the inscription has been set into the wall on the west side of the road below Bridgeness Tower.

Christian times

Round about A.D. 400, and as a result of Roman contacts, Christianity first came to Scotland and its gradual spread among four of the peoples who eventually went to make up the Scottish nation left its mark on some of our early monuments. Of these four peoples, three spoke different varieties of Celtic; the Britons in the south-west; the Picts, strongest in the north and east; and the Scots who had come from Ireland to Argyll and the Western Isles. Their form of Gaelic survives but, surprisingly, it was a Germanic language which ultimately became the language of government—that of a fourth race, the Anglo-Saxon Northumbrians who conquered the south and south-east. After much tribal fighting between the Picts and the Scots, these two were united in 843, under a Scottish king Kenneth MacAlpine, only to feel the impact, in the north and the west, of yet a fifth (and pagan) strain, that of the Scandinavian Norsemen. Of such a mixture was formed the Scotland of today.

The first Christian bishop that we know of was Ninian, who made his headquarters among the British at Whithorn, Wigtownshire, where there are some fifth- and sixth-century gravestones, one bearing the names of "two holy and excellent priests", Viventius and Maiorius.

The visible remains of the church and abbey, remarkable as they are, date only from the twelfth and the fifteenth centuries, but beneath them were found in 1945 what could well have been part of Ninian's Candida Casa, the white-walled monastery which he is said to have built there "of stone which is unusual among the Britons".

Another very early Christian relic—a memorial but hardly a monument—is of quite a different sort, a house-shaped casket or miniature shrine fashioned to contain a relic of, and to commemorate, a saint—in this case Columba who had come from Ireland as a missionary to Iona. It is ornamented with a dotted animal interlace pattern and gilded medallions set with red enamel, and is believed to date from the eighth century. It was formerly housed in the Abbey of Arbroath (Illustration 18), the foundation charter of which states that William the Lion (1165–1214) gave "the said Brecbennoch", or Blessed Shrine, and with it "the lands of Forglen given to God and St Columba and to the Brecbennoch, they making therefore the service in the army with the said Brecbennoch which is due to me from the said lands". Seven months after the Battle of Bannockburn, the then abbot who had been present at the battle, granted Forglen and the custody of the relic to Malcolm of Monymusk, from whose family it eventually passed to the Irvines of Drum and from them to the National Museum of Antiquities, Edinburgh. It is an Irish type of shrine but the animal ornament is paralleled in the St Ninian's Isle hoard and so is considered to be Pictish work. Also at the Battle of Bannockburn was the Abbot of Inchaffray who bore the Cross along the line of soldiers while:

The Scottis men, ful devotly
Knelit all don, til God to pray:
And a schort prayer thair maid thay
Til God to help them in that ficht.
And quhen the Inglis King had sicht
Of them kneland, he said in hy
"Yon folks knelis til ask mercy."
Schir Ingamo said "Ye say sooth now;
They ask mercy but not of yow.
For their trespass to God they cry.
I tell yow a thing sikkerly,
That yon men will win all or die."

There is nothing else of the same sort in Scotland but the crozier of St Fillan (National Museum of Antiquities) is also known to have been carried in that battle. This was brought back from Canada to where it had been taken by its hereditary custodians, the Dewar family, when they could no longer maintain themselves on the lands in Perthshire which went with it. It has silver panels of about 800 which have been at some time transferred on to a somewhat later case.

It was from Columba's Iona that missionaries first took Christianity to the Picts and to the Northumbrians.

The Picts

These were the people who left behind them by far the greatest number of interesting monuments from both before and after their conversion. From earlier, seventh-century days—the First Phase—there are unshaped slabs of stone with, incised on them, animals and symbols. Of the latter some are recognizable objects such as combs and mirrors; others, though they have no obvious identification, are so standardized as to be easily recognizable, such as the double circle and crescent, the Z-rod or the V.

With the coming of Christianity, three changes introduce a new phase; a cross appears on one side of the stone, usually embellished with interlacing patterns and sometimes with

5 a and b. Early Christian cross-slabs, fifth to sixth century, from
Whithorn, Wigtownshire. Left: The Roman lettering is beneath a cross
within a circle. The small hook attached to the upper arm of the cross
indicates that it represents a debased form of the early Christian sign for
Christ (Chi and Rho combined—the first two letters of the name in
Greek), and above the circle is carved an Alpha and (on its side) an
Omega for the First and Last. Right: Another stone, dedicated to St Peter,
has a more elegant cross made up of the arcs of circles; it also has the
Chi-Rho.

6 a and b, opposite: Phase I Pictish Stones. Left: From Meigle, Perthshire.
An incised stone showing a mirror symbol above and a grotesque beast
below. The museum here has the most representative collection of Phase I
and Phase II stones. Not far away, Aberlemno in Angus has others,
standing in the open, a fine Phase I stone by the roadside and some beautiful
Phase II ones in low relief, including, in the churchyard, that shown in
Illustration 7. Right: This stone, from Birsay in Orkney, does come from a
burial ground, but its direct association with the graves has been questioned.
It is, however, of great interest in that it combines incised symbols with
some low-relief carving, and because one of its symbols, the eagle, is

nowhere else found with the 'elephant' and the crescent with V-rod and the mirror-like symbol. There is also no cross on the other side as would have been expected, but this is probably due to its having been split off at some stage. It will be noted that the dress and equipment of the leading figure are grander than those of his two followers.

25

7 a and b. A Pictish cross-slab from Aberlemno. The interweaving patterns on the cross face may be compared with the rather different intersecting circles of the cross in Illustration 5b and with the West Highland patterns on the Kilmory Cross, Illustration 31. It has been suggested that a love of such decoration corresponds to the abstract, non-realistic or non-naturalistic cast of the Celtish mind as opposed to that of the more practical and humanistic Romans. The reverse side of this slab (right) carries typical Pictish symbols at the top and a lively group of men in battle below, mounted and on foot.

Biblical figures, though never with Christ on the Cross; the incised carving technique gives way to carving in relief; and the slabs themselves are now shaped. On the reverse side, and sometimes on the face itself, are spirited scenes of hunting and war. In a third phase, the shallow relief becomes deeper and the symbols disappear; the cross is more emphasized, per-haps because of Scottish influences.

Such stones bear so close a resemblance to modern grave-stones that it comes as something of a surprise that hardly any burials have been found in association with them, so that various other explanations have been suggested as to what may have been the purpose behind their erection. These include the commemoration of wedding alliances (partly because symbols are hardly ever found singly), boundary stones giving evidence of personal possession, and memorials (on the analogy of the Nelson Column) unassociated with burials; but none of the theories has been supported by suf-ficient evidence to win general acceptance.[1]

Distribution maps in *An Historical Atlas of Scotland c. 400–c. 1600*, edited by P. McNeill and R. Nicholson, show the greatest concentration of Phase I stones in the north-east; of Phase II in Strathmore; and of Phase III there and in Fife. In the National Museum of Antiquities, a collection of originals and casts provides an unrivalled opportunity to follow the development of the art form and there are collections at Meigle, Perthshire, and St Vigeans, Angus. They display not only the skill of the carvers and the beauty of the finished products but the wealth of historical information that can be gleaned from them:

> They illustrate the most ancient life in Scotland of which we have any illustrations. They show it in its most common as well as in its ecclesiastical and military aspects. They exhibit the dress of the huntsman, the warrior, the pilgrim, and the ecclesiastic. They furnish representations of the chariot, and the ship, the housings and harness of horses, instruments of music, arms of offence and defence, the staff of the pilgrim and the crosier of the ecclesiastic. . . . Customs and fashions of which there is no other distinct evidence are also

---

[1] The matter is further complicated by the fact that few can now be in their original locations.

represented. For instance, we learn that the horsemen of that period rode without stirrups, cropped the manes and the tails of their horses, used snaffle-bridles with cheek-rings and ornamental rosettes, and sat upon peaked saddle-cloths; that, when journeying on horseback, they wore peaked hoods and cloaks, and, when hunting or on horseback, armed, they wore a kilt-like dress, falling below mid-thighs, and a plaid across the shoulders . . . that when journeying on foot they wore trews or tight-fitting nether-garments . . . that they wore their hair long, flowing, and curly, sometimes with peaked beards, at other times with moustaches on the upper lip and shaven cheeks and chin . . . that they used chairs with side-arms and high curved backs, sometimes ornamented with the heads of animals; that their boats had high prows and stern-posts; that the long dresses of their ecclesiastics were richly embroidered; that they walked in loose short boots, and carried crosiers and book-satchels.[2]

The author might have added that the carvings were so faithful that it has been possible to identify two separate breeds of dogs, and two of horses.

The third phase of Pictish carving, where the sculpture is in much higher relief, may be seen in the Cathedral Museum at St Andrews on a stone sarcophagus, the carving of which is remarkable for its delicacy and vigour. Among the scenes displayed is one of David rending a lion. Snake-like inter-twined animals and bosses show the beginnings of Scottish influence from the west (compare Illustration 10).

J. S. Richardson in *The Medieval Scottish Carver in Stone*, Edinburgh University Press, 1964, has some interesting pages in his first chapter on the methods used by the early carvers.

Before turning to Northumbrian and Scottish monuments, one last (possibly) Pictish memorial may be mentioned. In the year 685, while the Picts were still pagan, their king Brude

[2] J. Anderson: *Scotland in Early Christian Times.*

8. Restenneth Abbey.

finally stemmed the attempts by the Northumbrians to advance northwards at the Battle of Nechtansmere, near Forfar. Twenty-five years later, his son Nechtan accepted Christianity and, on his baptism, ordered a church to be built. It has been suggested that this was at Restenneth, the site traditionally associated with the event. Most of the buildings that survive on that lovely unspoilt site in Strathmore are those of a twelfth-century monastery, but the lowest section of the tower, and the doorway with its high single-stone arch, are certainly very much older and may go back to the days of Nechtan himself.

The Northumbrian influence in southern Scotland

Far the finest example is the great cross, now preserved in a chapel specially built for it in the church of Ruthwell, Dumfriesshire, dating from around 750. This stands 17½ feet high, and is 2 feet wide and over one foot thick. On the broad sides are carved, most beautifully, a number of Biblical scenes which are identified by inscriptions in Latin; on the edge, or thinner side, is a characteristic Northumbrian pattern formed by a vine with birds feeding on its fruit and, in vertical columns, a Runic inscription. The story of the decipherment of this last, as told in Anderson's *Scotland in Early Christian Times*, makes an entertaining warning to students. The first decipherer,

> Mr Repp transliterated the inscription, and extracted from it a singularly distinct and coherent record of the donation of a baptismal font of eleven pounds weight, with its ornaments, by authority of the Therfusian Fathers, in expiation for the devastation of the fields and the spoliation of thirteen cows in the vale of Ashlafar.

Unfortunately, although he had in most cases read the letters correctly, he had extracted a totally false meaning from them by misinterpreting the language in which they were written to be a dialect of old Norse. In fact, the language was Anglo-Saxon and the inscription was part of a poem about Christ on the Rood, possibly by Caedmon.[3]

Of the carvings, those of the healing of the blind man, and the anointing of Jesus's feet by Mary Magdalene, may be seen in the illustration. On the reverse are the Flight into Egypt, the meeting of Saints Paul and Anthony in the desert, the triumph of Jesus over the wild beasts, and St John the Baptist.

The Scots

The achievement of the Scots at this early stage was much influenced by the artistic traditions of Ireland whence they came and especially by their High Crosses which are thought

---

[3] Readers of Scott may remember a similar incident in *The Antiquary*, where *Agricola dicavit libens lubens* became "Aiken Drum's lang ladle".

9. The Ruthwell Cross.

10. *The Kildalton Cross, Islay. Made in the ninth century out of a single slab of local bluestone, it has the typical open circle or wheel-shaped head which is Celtic and the characteristic bosses which derive from metalwork, just as the spiral patterns derive from contemporary manuscripts. On the other hand, the vine pattern on the sides of the cross more nearly resembles Northumbrian work.*

to mark the sites of preaching places; some of them however may also have been memorials to individuals such as that of Abbot Muiredach who died at Monasterboice, County Louth, in 923. The finest Scottish examples are those of Kildalton in the Island of Islay and St Martin's Cross in Iona.

These early crosses do not bear the figure of Christ crucified but may include other groups of figures on the arms of the cross. At Kildalton they include the Virgin and Child (who also occur on the St Martin's Cross but in the centre—in this case the wheel is smaller in proportion to the shaft, giving a more graceful effect). The fragments of a third great cross, that of St John from Iona, are in the National Museum and a replica has been erected in Iona.

The fusion of the peoples

If the first step was the acquisition by the Scottish king, Kenneth MacAlpine, either by force or by some hereditary claim, of the kingdom of the Picts, the trend must have been strengthened by the external threat posed by the Vikings. Kenneth must have been the more glad to move his head-quarters from Dunadd in Argyll to the centre of Perthshire, in that it was the islands and the sea-lochs of the west which were especially subject to the raids of the Norsemen. Illustrations I and II may well be a commentary on this new threat.

At Forres stands a vast pillar 23 feet high, 4 feet wide and over a foot thick. In low relief on one side is a wheel-cross with interlacing pattern, and on the flanks are entwined beasts and foliage of Northumbrian origin. But it is the reverse which is unique: it is covered with groups of figures which to the layman make it obvious that it is a commemoration of a victory in war—it has been suggested that it might be of the Scandinavian Sweyn over Malcolm II in 1008 but this is probably too late. Dr W. Douglas Simpson has lent weight to the possibility that the stone does depict a secular victory but one of a native force over an invader, which in many ways seems more probable. He writes in *The Ancient Stones of Scotland*:

On the back of the slab is an astonishing array of closely marshalled military scenes; infantry and cavalry in martial posture or arranged in actual combat, rows of headless corpses laid out as if for counting—the whole set forth with a deliberate ruthlessness that reminds one of Assyrian bas-reliefs, and has no parallel among the Celtic monuments of Britain and Ireland. In the middle of this grim sequence is carved an object shaped like a flat-topped or truncated cone, with a door at ground level in front. This door has sloping jambs in the Celtic manner. Dr James Richardson, to whose sharp and well-trained eye Scottish archaeology owes so much, has suggested that this subject is the portrayal of a broch. Upon the whole, it seems hard to escape the conclusion that all this sculpture on the reverse of Sueno's Stone depicts an actual historical event—a victorious battle which the monument was erected to commemorate. That it was a victory over Norse invaders is suggested by the name "Sueno's Stone", attached to the monument since immemorial times. And that a broch plays its part in the campaign is in no way unlikely, for we know from the Sagas that the Broch of Mousa figured in events in 900 and 1153, in which latter year it stood a siege.

Pressure from the Norsemen

Scotland, like Ireland and England, had to withstand an influx of Scandinavians; some were warlike plunderers such as those who pillaged Iona but many were peaceable peasants escaping from an overpopulated homeland. Settling in the islands, and in Caithness and Sutherland, they added to the amalgam of races. Ireland has many round towers built in the tenth to the twelfth centuries as bell towers, for early warning against invaders and for refuge. Mainland Scotland has two such towers, one at Abernethy on the borders of Perthshire and Fife, and the one illustrated at Brechin.

11. The Round Tower at Brechin, circa A.D. 1000. The doorway, with its border and its round-headed arch made of a single stone, is typical of the Irish towers. There is a crucifix over the door with Christ's legs uncrossed—a subject not shown on Pictish or Scottish crosses of that date. On either side are clerics, one with the curved Celtic pastoral staff, one with the much older T-shaped Coptic staff.

Inside the cathedral there is a hog-back tombstone of Scandinavian type with carvings of priests and animals, and a Pictish cross-slab.

12. *A tomb in Dundrennan Abbey, Kirkcudbright, founded in 1142. Its ruins include much lovely work from the twelfth and thirteenth centuries, and the tombs of a Swinton c.1200 and of Devorguilla of Galloway's parents, Margaret and Alan, c.1250. But the most interesting and the best preserved tomb is that of this Cistercian abbot. His right hand holds a dagger, and at his feet lies a gruesome little figure with its bowels protruding, signifying, it is thought, that the abbot had been murdered by someone who disliked the importation of foreign monks from Rievaulx.*

TWO

The House of Canmore,
1050–1290

Kenneth MacAlpine and his successors found themselves unable to prevent the Norsemen (who already ruled Shetland and Orkney) from establishing themselves also in the Western Isles, but the Scottish kings did add to their dominions southwards. Malcolm II, 1005–34, conquered the Lothians and Strathclyde with the result that his grandson Duncan, 1034–40, was king over the whole of mainland Scotland as we know it. He was quite unlike Shakespeare's picture of him— "not a good old king but a headstrong young one" and he was incompetent into the bargain; one of the reasons for his deposition and death in battle at the hands of Macbeth was his failure in an attempt to acquire Northumbrian lands south of what was later to become the Border. Macbeth, 1040–57, was defeated at Lumphanan by Duncan's son Malcolm III, 1057–93, "Canmore".

A big change came when Canmore married as his second wife a bride who was Anglo-Saxon by birth and Hungarian by upbringing; change in ecclesiastical organization, in art and architecture, and eventually in language. The Roman Use was enforced for the Mass; bishops were given far greater authority in the Church and, in due course, in the secular government too; dioceses and parishes were organized; and the hub of religious life was moved again—first to Dunfermline (Margaret's preferred home, where she and her husband were buried) and then to St Andrews. Romanesque methods of building were introduced from the south, and Norman and Breton barons were encouraged by grants of land to settle in Scotland, bringing with them feudal ideas of administration. But the French language which they spoke did not prevail here any more than it did in England. Nor, somewhat surprisingly, did Gaelic which was the tongue of the Royal House and of the majority of the subjects. Instead, a form of English spread as the southern Lowlands became increasingly the richest and the dominant section of the country, where towns developed as centres of distribution and trade.

Margaret and her husband were a remarkable couple. He was a man of his age—at least as ruthless as most. The orders that he gave after hearing of a Northumbrian incursion into his southern borders were to spare none of the English on whom his men could lay hands. The old men and women were to be slaughtered "like swine for a banquet"; the young men and maidens—indeed all who might be useful as slaves—were driven away into a land of bondage. As for Margaret, it was one of her achievements that she was later able to mitigate the lot of some of the victims. Her greatest achievement was to humanize the King whom she had only married under compulsion, when she had hoped to devote her life to prayer in a nunnery. She never taught him to read but she inspired him with a respect for the books she loved; indeed, those she most treasured, he would pore over and kiss. And "sometimes he sent for a worker in precious metals whom he would command to ornament that volume with gold and gems, and, when it was finished, the King himself would carry the volume to the Queen as a kind of proof of his devotion". She persuaded him to join her in her Maundy washing of the feet of twenty-four poor persons, and in her night-time devotions, and in her charitable giving; and she so instructed him that, using the English which he had learnt as a boy at the English court, he was able to act as interpreter between the priests whom Margaret imported from England and the Gaelic-speaking clergy of Scotland. Turgot's *Life of Margaret* makes her sound a solemn and formidable ascetic, but she can hardly have been such or she would never have managed to keep the affection of such a man as Malcolm nor to have won from him such loving tolerance, even when she dipped her fingers into his purse (and his wardrobe) for her constant gifts to the poor. Nor would she have won her way in persuading the Scottish church to accept so many reforms that must have been unpalatable. Nor would her sons have followed so closely in her footsteps rather than have reacted against their up-bringing.

Iona was one of the places which benefited from the new life that she brought to native monasticism. Columba's Celtic abbey had been repeatedly sacked by Norse raiders until the remaining monks had eventually to depart for Ireland. Margaret refounded the abbey as a Benedictine outpost. The only building surviving that may belong to her day is the eleventh-century chapel of St Oran in the centre of Illustration 13. The restored abbey church, behind, was begun around 1204 by Somerled; in front is the Relig Oran where Scottish kings used to be buried, and also the island chiefs, the MacDonalds, the Macleans and the MacLeods among them. "This sanctuary," wrote Dean Monro just before the Reformation, "was wont to be the sepulture of the best men of all the iles, and also of our kings,[1] as we have said; because it was the most honorable and ancient place, that was in Scotland in thair days, as we reid." Since this photograph was taken, most of the stones shown have been removed to a museum within the abbey precincts to preserve them. None of the early kings nor of the Lords of the Isles can now be identified but one twelfth-century stone could be that of Godfrey, Norse King of Man.

---

[1] Malcolm Canmore was the first Scottish king not to be buried in Iona. After him, only one king was buried there—his brother and short-lived successor, Donaldbane, 1093-7.

13. St Oran's Chapel, Iona, in the foreground. Oran was a friend of Columba and may even have been on Iona before him. So deeply did Columba love him that he could not bear to be present at his death—a story much more probable than the oft-quoted legend that, when the two were speculating about life after death, Oran offered to be buried alive so that he might learn for certain what it was like. Unfortunately (the story goes) when he was dug up again after three days, he so shocked Columba by declaring that the conventional teaching of the Church was all wrong and that neither were the good eternally happy nor the bad forever consumed by fire that Columba had him hurriedly covered up again before he could utter any more dangerous heresy.

14. A grave-slab from Iona. The ship and the hammer and tongs forging a sword could be a reference to the story of Sigurd, and it has been suggested that this may have been a memorial to Godfrey, King of Man, who was buried on Iona in the twelfth century.

15. *Dunfermline Abbey. The massive pillars and severe round arches, ornamented only with plain zigzag, give the impression of strength rather than beauty. But there is beauty to be found, once your eyes have accustomed themselves to the dim light, especially in the arcading round the walls. On the floor the outlines of the earlier churches are indicated by an inlaid brass strip. There are fine remains of later monastic buildings and of a royal palace. The complex as a whole can be best seen from the gardens of Pittencrieff Park—itself a memorial to Andrew Carnegie.*

16. *St Margaret's Chapel, Edinburgh Castle, is all that remains of the earliest castle on the rock in Edinburgh. Tradition claims that it was built by Margaret herself and that she worshipped and heard her last Mass here in 1093, but the chancel arch and the apse are more likely to date from David I's time. The outer doorway and the vault of the nave are modern.*

Margaret built a considerable church at Dunfermline for the Benedictine monastery which she founded there, where she and her husband were buried but all that remains of her church are its foundations and, of her tomb, its plain base. Her true monument is not her tomb but the great Romanesque nave which her youngest son David I, 1124–53, built as a memorial to his parents, using masons trained at Durham.

Other churches which were built specifically as memorials include Sweetheart Abbey in Kirkcudbrightshire (Illustration 19) and the cathedral of St Magnus, Kirkwall, Orkney.

David I was considered by his successors to have been a "sair saint for the crown" but much that he did was later of use to them in their administration of the realm. He and they continued the introduction of Norman and Breton families—Balliol, Bruce, Stewart, Wallace, and Douglas among others, all to be doughty Scottish patriots in due course, even if at

17. *The aisle of St Magnus Cathedral, Kirkwall, Orkney. Of the same date as Dundrennan, but still Romanesque in style, is the nave of this church, started by the Norse Earl Rognvald in memory of his kinsman Magnus. The latter had been martyred on the island of Egilsay, only twenty-one years before, by order of Earl Haakon. In a cavity in one of the pillars on the north side of the nave—eight feet six inches above ground— were found remains which may well have been Rognvald's. There is much of great interest in the cathedral, which is impressive out of all proportion to its size, especially the carving on the capitals, the doorways and the tombstones which have been arranged round the walls. These include one of Adam Stewart, a son of James V.*

times a thorn in the side of the monarch. No doubt part of the reason was to counterbalance the more powerful of the older established families—those of Galloway in particular, and of the Norsemen, and the half-Norse Somerled, all of whom were reluctant to give up their semi-independence. David's elder grandson Malcolm IV, 1153–65, suffered especially at their hands.

And, of course, neither Malcolm IV nor William the Lion, 1165–1214, could rival in strength the kings of England to whom they, from time to time, paid homage and even occasionally followed in battle. Whether the homage was paid, as the English claimed, for Scotland, or because they were also owners of extensive holdings in England—such as the Earldom of Huntingdon—was a moot point. Malcolm died young, but William, after a disastrous start when he was defeated in battle at Alnwick and had to endure a long detention at the court of Henry II (where he became a friend of Becket), proved himself a vigorous and effective ruler, successful in restoring internal peace and in encouraging trade and the growth of towns.

Arbroath Abbey may be regarded as a monument to the spirit of the Scottish nation that a hundred years later was being forged by the necessity of resistance to the attacks of the English. It was the Abbot of Arbroath who in 1320 drafted the Declaration, on behalf of the great men of the realm, that the Scots would support their king against all men, so long as he should be true:

> Yet if he should give up what he has begun, seeking to make us, or our Kingdom, subject to the King of England or to the English, we would strive at once to drive him out as our enemy and subverter of his own rights and ours and we would make some other man, who was able to defend us, our king, for, so long as a hundred of us remain alive we will never on any conditions be subjected to the lordship of the English. For we fight not for glory, nor riches, nor honours, but for freedom alone, which no good man gives up but with his life.

18. *Arbroath Abbey. Begun by William the Lion as his personal memorial to Thomas à Becket only eight years after his martyrdom, it was also intended to be William's own memorial, and he was buried there before the High Altar in 1214. Architecturally, the church is of interest because, contrary to what one would expect, the earlier part, the east end, is more developed in style with its pointed arches than the later Romanesque west doorway. In the museum are a number of interesting monuments but nothing to compare with the lower part of the effigy that adorned William's tomb chest, one of the very earliest Scottish effigies to survive. He is clad in his coronation robes, a long tunic girded at the waist and, over it, his imperial mantle held back by a number of little figures of knights in chain mail. The feet rest upon a lion. The carving is likely to be either English or French.*

45

But for the time being it was trouble nearer home that was the more pressing. Alexander II, 1214–49, had to fight in Galloway and he died on Kerrera off Oban Bay leading a great naval expedition against the influence of the King of Norway and his subjects the King of Man and the Earl of Orkney. When the latter retaliated, Alexander III, 1249–86,—and a great storm—combined to end the Norse power in Scotland for ever at Largs in 1263. In 1265 Norway ceded all her Scottish possessions except the Northern Isles, and peace was cemented by the marriage of Alexander III's daughter. She died in 1283 and Alexander in 1286—killed by a fall from his horse. The modern memorial to him at Kinghorn is undistinguished but its situation on the cliffs is fine.

The twelfth and thirteenth centuries were a period of extensive religious building as the kings and their subjects hastened to endow monasteries for the wealthy international orders—Benedictine, Cluniac, Tironensian, Cistercian, Augustinian, Premonstratensian and Valliscaulian. New Abbey near Dumfries was a Cistercian foundation which was specifically a memorial.

Some of the monumental sculpture of this period was outstanding, though sadly not much remains. An early example is a dignified figure of a thirteenth-century Cistercian abbot at Dundrennan. With it may be compared a headless effigy of a Bishop of Moray at Elgin—approximately contemporary— of which Dr J. S. Richardson has written:

> Another effigy is one which was found some years ago buried in the graveyard on the north side of the Cathedral of the Bishop of Moray near the west re-entrant angle of the Chapter House, where it had apparently been reverently reburied after it had been destroyed by the fire of 1390. Unfortunately, in digging a grave in later times part of this effigy had been broken off and removed. A thirteenth-century bishop is portrayed with extraordinary fidelity of visage and vestment, and on the effigy are still to be seen traces of colour treatment. The arrangement of the figure

19. New or 'Sweetheart' Abbey. Devorguilla, heiress to Alan, last of the old Celtic line of Galloway, married the incomer John Balliol the elder (see Genealogical Table on page 50). When he died, she founded this monastery in his memory. Only the church survives, its Decorated architecture set off by its lovely setting. Its popular name derives from the request of the foundress that she should be buried before the High Altar with her husband's sweet heart embalmed and resting on her own. The fragments of her effigy which have been gathered together in the south transept are those of a sixteenth-century replacement of the original. Beside them lies the decorated coffin lid of John, the first abbot, c.1300.

and the position of the right hand, raised in blessing, the left holding the pastoral staff, the low precious mitre, the elegantly arranged folds of a soft chasuble of full material, and the enrichments on the material apparels of the stoles and alb suggest a date towards the middle of the thirteenth century. The possibility that this extremely important example of sculpture may represent Andrew de Moravia, who founded the Cathedral in 1224, should not be over-looked. The face of the Bishop is beautifully rendered, the eyes with their arched eyebrows being in accord with these features on the Christ head at St Andrews. The gentle modelling of the features and the treatment of the mous-tache and the beard also show a similarity to the St Andrews carving. One is almost tempted to suggest that these two masterpieces are the work of the same man. There is at this same cathedral the headless figure of another bishop which has come from an ornate tomb—namely that of Bishop John Innes. The great importance of this particular figure in Scottish medieval monumental sculpture has been so far overlooked. The large-scale image, vested in alb and cope, is shown kneeling on a cushion in the attitude of prayer. From a designer's point of view a cope is more agreeable to the portrayal of such a posture than would be ecclesiastic vestments. A kneeling figure has naturally to be free-stand-ing, and therefore it has to be complete on every side in all its details. The alb, bound at the waist, falls in carefully arranged folds and those of the cope sweep down and away, following the kneeling profile. The pastoral staff has passed under the left gloved wrist, and the ornate head, now lost, has projected over the left shoulder. Bishop Innes was consecrated at Avignon in 1406 by Benedict XIII, the anti-pope, and he died in 1414. The record tablet from his tomb tells us that for seven years he was engaged in building notable work at his cathedral, and certainly from the architectural features which bespeak his endeavours in that direction, and also judging from the existing fragments of his tomb, he employed a first-class master mason. No doubt when this bishop was abroad the kneeling figures in monumental work introduced by the Italian Classic Renaissance architects appealed to his mind and therefore we can accept that he selected this particular pose for the figure of his own tomb, which was made in his lifetime. From the clue thus provided by this bishop's effigy we can state with certainty that Bishop Kennedy of St Andrews, who when in Florence had also viewed the Renaissance monuments, selected a similar kneeling position for the figure of himself, a necessary feature in his most magnificent tomb which is the adornment of the College chapel he founded at St Andrews. Kennedy died in 1465 and his tomb [see Illustration 43], with its rich overhead celestial Jerusalem and Tournay marble tomb-chest, once richly ornamented on the front with brasswork of Flemish manufacture, was ordered and made during his lifetime. Have we not reason to believe that this contract was arranged and put in hand before the building of his College kirk, and that the original intention was that this superlative work of monumental quality was devised originally for a place within an arch in the great cathedral where the delicate pinnacles could reach upwards towards the triforium? This suggestion is borne out by the fact that the return ends of the monument show a display of niches for statuettes which in their present position are lost.

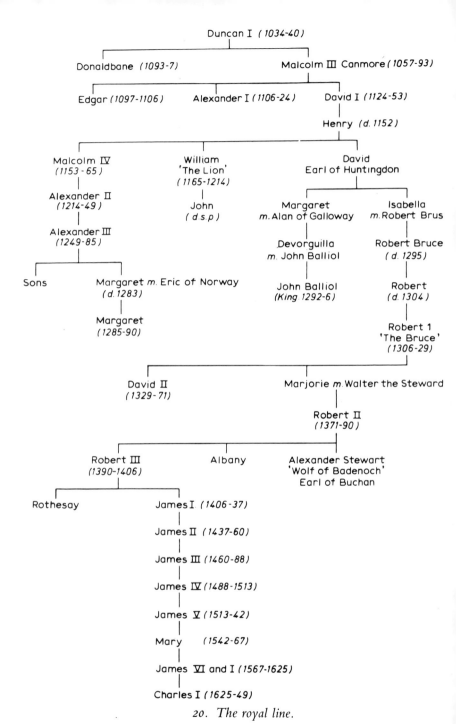

Duncan I *(1034-40)*

Donaldbane *(1093-7)*   Malcolm III Canmore *(1057-93)*

Edgar *(1097-1106)*   Alexander I *(1106-24)*   David I *(1124-53)*

Henry *(d. 1152)*

Malcolm IV *(1153-65)*   William 'The Lion' *(1165-1214)*   David Earl of Huntingdon

Alexander II *(1214-49)*   John *(d.s.p)*

Alexander III *(1249-85)*   Margaret m. Alan of Galloway   Isabella m. Robert Brus

Sons   Margaret m. Eric of Norway *(d.1283)*   Devorguilla m. John Balliol   Robert Bruce *(d. 1295)*

Margaret *(1285-90)*   John Balliol *(King. 1292-6)*   Robert *(d. 1304)*

Robert 1 'The Bruce' *(1306-29)*

David II *(1329-71)*   Marjorie m. Walter the Steward

Robert II *(1371-90)*

Robert III *(1390-1406)*   Albany   Alexander Stewart 'Wolf of Badenoch' Earl of Buchan

Rothesay   James I *(1406-37)*

James II *(1437-60)*

James III *(1460-88)*

James IV *(1488-1513)*

James V *(1513-42)*

Mary   *(1542-67)*

James VI and I *(1567-1625)*

Charles I *(1625-49)*

20. The royal line.

THREE

The Disputed Succession
and the Wars
against England, 1300–1406

With the death of Alexander III, the House of Canmore is sometimes said to have come to an end, but in fact every sovereign since his day has been descended from Malcolm through a younger brother of William the Lion.[1]

All Alexander's children had predeceased him and his only descendant was his infant granddaughter, the Maid of Norway. Her mother had been married to the king of that country, an event marred by the sinking, on the return journey, of a ship carrying some of the nobles who had been sent to escort her. This disaster gave rise to "The ballad of Sir Patrick Spens":

The King sits in Dunfermline town
    Drinking the blude-red wine;
"O where will I get a skeely skipper
    To sail this new ship o' mine?"

O up and spake an eldern knight,
    Sat at the king's right knee;
"Sir Patrick Spens is the best sailor
    That ever sailed the sea."

[1] William the Lion was buried at Arbroath (see page 45).

51

Our king has written a braid letter,
    And sealed it with his hand,
And sent it to Sir Patrick Spens,
    Was walking on the strand.

"To Noroway, to Noroway,
    To Noroway o'er the faem:
The King's daughter of Noroway,
    'Tis thou must bring her hame."

The first word that Sir Patrick read
    So loud, loud laughed he;
The next word that Sir Patrick read
    The tear blinded his e'e.

"O wha is this has done this deed
    And told the king of me,
To send us out, at this time o' year,
    To sail upon the sea?

Be it wind, be it weet, be it hail, be it sleet,
    Our ship must sail the faem;
The king's daughter o' Noroway,
    'Tis we must bring her hame."

They hoysed their sails on Monenday morn
    With a' the speed they may;
They hae landed in Noroway
    Upon a Wodensday.

The Return

"Mak ready, mak ready, my merry men a';
    Our good ship sails the morn."
"Now ever alack, my master dear,
    I fear a deadly storm."

"I saw the new moon late yestreen
    Wi' the old moon in her arm;
And if we gang to sea, master,
    I fear we'll come to harm."

They hadna' sailed a league, a league,
    A league but barely three,

When the lift grew dark, and the wind blew loud,
  And gurly grew the sea.

The ankers brake, and the topmast lap,
  It was sic a deadly storm;
And the waves cam owre the broken ship
  Till a' her sides were torn.

"Go fetch a web o' the silken cloth,
  Another o' the twine,
And wap them into our ship's side,
  And let nae the sea come in."

They fetched a web o' the silken cloth,
  Another o' the twine,
And they wapp'd them round the good ship's side
  But still the sea came in.

O laith, laith were our gude Scots lords
  To wet their cork-heeled shoon;
But lang or a' the play was played
  They wet their hats aboon.

And mony was the feather-bed
  That flattered on the faem;
And mony was the gude lord's son
  That never mair came hame.

O lang, lang may the ladies sit,
  Wi' their fans into their hand,
Before they see Sir Patrick Spens
  Come sailing to the strand!

And lang, lang may the maidens sit
  With their gowd kames in their hair,
A-waiting for their ane dear loves!
  For them they'll see nae mair.

Half-owre, half-owre to Aberdour,
  'Tis fifty fathoms deep;
And there lies gude Sir Patrick Spens,
  Wi' the Scots lords at his feet.

The fact that Scotland had no king, only an infant queen, prompted the English king to use the situation to unite the two kingdoms by securing the betrothal of the infant to his own young son and heir. He even sought to gain possession of her by sending a magnificently equipped ship to fetch her from Norway, "well-stored with luxuries—thirty-one hogsheads and one pipe of wine, ten barrels of beer and a large quantity of salt beef, hams, dried fish, stock fish, lampreys, sturgeon, and fifty pounds of whale; along with twenty-two gallons of mustard, salt, pepper, vinegar and onions, with a little stock of dainties for the delicate stomach of the young princess—consisting of five hundred walnuts, two loaves of sugar, grits and oatmeal, mace, figs, raisins and thirty-eight pounds of gingerbread". Proudly but wisely the King of Norway declined, saying that a Norwegian princess should sail only in a Norwegian ship. But it made little difference; the child died on the voyage and was buried in Orkney. One of those who had escorted the child's mother to Norway had been Walter Stewart, Earl of Menteith, whose tomb is at Inchmahome

*21. The tomb of the Earl and Countess of Menteith, Inchmahome Priory. "Even in decay" this "remains one of the most expressive and moving stone monuments in Scotland. . . . Mutilated though it may be, deprived of its canopy, worn by the elements, and with all trace of its colour gone from its grey freestone, the work retains rhythmic line and sculptural unity" (*Late Monumental Sculpture in the West Highlands, K. A. Steer and J. W. M. Bannerman, Royal Commission on the Ancient and Historical Monuments of Scotland*). The Earl is in the act of turning over towards his wife (who predeceased him)—unlike the majority of such tombs, here husband and wife do not lie apart gazing into the skies as though unaware of each other—his left arm is reaching over to take her hand, his right lies beneath her head, as hers does beneath his; and her head is half turned towards him. No photograph can do justice to this piece of statuary.*

Also at Inchmahome are another Stewart effigy and a grave-slab c.1360 of Sir John Drummond, carved in low relief. He wears a tall helmet with a cross on top and is girt with a large shield, sword and knife. On either side of his head are small figures, one of a bishop and one of St Michael with the dragon. The priory was founded for the Cistercians by the Earl's brother-in-law (and predecessor as Earl of Menteith) and was a refuge for Mary, Queen of Scots, as an infant.

Priory in the Lake of Menteith. Earlier he had been on a Crusade and had also fought at the Battle of Largs against King Haakon of Norway. He died in 1294.

A number of people laid claim to the throne but only two were seriously considered, both descended from William the Lion's younger brother, the Earl of Huntingdon. One was John Balliol, son of the founder of Sweetheart Abbey; the other, Robert Bruce; and when the King of England, Edward I, was asked to adjudicate, it was Balliol whom he chose. Seeing it as a chance to force a subordinate status on the Scots, Edward piled indignities on Balliol, so that when the leading Scots forced Balliol to resist, Edward could invade the land, defeat its armies and take Balliol (and the Stone of Destiny on which Scottish kings used to be enthroned) back to London. He left behind him Englishmen to govern a country which he thought had been conquered for all time. It was left to two men (who differed considerably in background) to lead the resistance in turn.

The ancestors of William Wallace may originally have come from Wales, as those of Bruce came from Normandy, via England, but by the thirteenth century they held no lands outside Scotland, and no great estates even there. And William had taken no oaths of allegiance to Edward as Bruce and many of the greater nobles had. The ascendancy that this member of the lesser gentry acquired was due solely to his courage and personality and skill as a guerrilla fighter. Wallace brought in the strength of the south, and Andrew de Moray that of the north. When Edward sent the Earl of Surrey to reduce them, they defeated him by catching the English army while it was still in the process of crossing the river at the old bridge of Stirling.

After Stirling, Wallace was knighted and made Guardian of the Realm on behalf of Balliol, but lacking the support of the greater lords, many of whom had lands in England and divided loyalties, he was defeated when he allowed himself to be drawn into a pitched battle at Falkirk. Later he was betrayed and taken to London where he was barbarously executed as a traitor to a King he had never acknowledged. Already a hero to his fellow countrymen he now became a martyr. His best-known monuments are Victorian (see Illustration 86).

Bruce, on the other hand, did hold lands in England and had made submission to Edward, but now he saw in the failure and deposition of Balliol, and in the strong national feeling aroused and given shape by Wallace's life and by his death, an opportunity both to deliver Scotland from her oppressors and to gain the crown for himself. Nevertheless, what finally caused him to set out on a course from which there was no turning back was an affray—and here there is a point of similarity between him and Wallace. It is said that what started Wallace on his desperate adventure was his outlawry as a result of his killing the Sheriff of Lanark, who had caused to be executed a girl who had helped him to escape when he became involved in a scuffle with some English soldiers. Bruce, as is well known, was outlawed and excommunicated as a result of killing John the Red Comyn on 10th February 1306 in the Greyfriars' Church at Dumfries. Such an act might well have proved disastrous by losing him the support not only of the north-east from which the Comyns drew considerable strength, and of all the Balliol supporters, because the Red Comyn was a nephew of Balliol, and of the MacDougalls in the west, who were likewise closely related, but also of the Church. In fact, when Bruce proceeded straight to Scone to get himself acknowledged as King, the Abbot supported him, as did the Bishops of St Andrews, Glasgow and Moray; and when the Earl of Fife was not available to place the crown on his head (as was his hereditary right) his sister, the Countess of Buchan, courageously did so, and paid heavily; when she was later captured by the English she was kept for four years in a cage. However successful Bruce was in getting himself acknowledged, everything else went awry. In June 1306 his small forces were beaten at Methven and for two years he was a fugitive mostly in the Highlands, and his wife and daughter Marjorie were taken prisoners. To this period belong the well-known stories of the spider which he watched trying,

22 a and b. Incised slabs from the tombs of Sir William Oliphant at Aberdalgie, Perth, and David Barclay, Creich, Fife, c.1400.

The Oliphant tomb used to stand in an earlier church and then, when that became roofless, in the open, and it has suffered accordingly. The knight lies in armour beneath a canopy, the sides of which once had six smaller figures. On the shield beside his head are the three crescents of the Oliphants. He died in 1329. The tomb is described in detail and the question of attribution discussed by F. A. Greenhill in Proceedings of the Society of the Antiquaries of Scotland, 1946.

The Barclay slab (right) is later, David having died in 1400 and his wife in 1421; their faces are sunk, apparently to receive alabaster or marble inlays. It has been removed for protection from the old to the new church. It is referred to in P.S.A.S. 1899–1900, as is another remarkable slab from Longforgan Church, Angus. See also P.S.A.S. 1908–9 for a description of slabs at Foveran Aberdeenshire (two Knights fourteenth century) and Oathlaw (a priest, rather later).

time and time again, to climb up its slender thread until it eventually succeeded; of the Brooch of Lorne which a MacDougall snatched from his plaid as he just succeeded in making his escape, and the Ugadale Brooch which he gave to one who had succoured him after only the warmth of a goat, to which he had clung all night, had saved him from dying of exposure; and of the occasion on which John MacDougall of Lorne was pursuing him with bloodhounds and he had to divide his party repeatedly to try to throw the beasts off the scent; but each time it was picked up again until only one companion was left with him and both had to take to the water to save themselves.

For Bruce, the tide turned only when Edward I died and when he was able to defeat the Comyn party at Inverurie, and then the MacDougalls in the Pass of Brander in 1308. There remained the English to be driven out but gradually one town after another was retaken, the culmination coming when Edward II tried to relieve Stirling before it succumbed to the fate that by 1314 had overtaken all to the north of it, and also Edinburgh and Roxburgh. The skilful use of ground at Bannockburn enabled a complete victory over an army stronger in both cavalry and infantry.

When Robert I died in 1329, he was buried at Dunfermline in an elaborate tomb but this has perished except for a few fragments which are in the National Museum of Antiquities in Edinburgh; the brass over his grave in the Abbey is late Victorian, but simple and dignified. And there are other Victorian memorials to the most famous of Scottish kings, and a 1929 statue (rather exaggeratedly determined) on the gateway to Edinburgh Castle. His best memorial is that at Bannockburn itself, unveiled by Her Majesty the Queen in 1964 (see Illustration 93).

There is, however, a contemporary tomb of a Sir William Oliphant, probably the one who was the founder of the great Jacobite family of Oliphants and one of Bruce's friends. This one had commanded the little garrison of Stirling when it had been besieged by Edward I, and he had held out for twelve months before the castle was finally forced to yield and he was sent as a prisoner to the Tower of London. Thereafter, he is found defending Perth for the English against Bruce, but he changed sides again to fight *for* him at Bannockburn and to sign the Declaration of Arbroath.

During the years of strife between the houses of Balliol and of Bruce, and between Scotland and England, Bruce had received the support of, amongst others, the MacDonald Lords of the Isles, based at this time in Islay; of Sir Niall Campbell of Argyll; and of the Douglases from the Borders, though each of these families was in due course to become a serious threat to the monarchy that they had helped to establish.

When Robert I died and was succeeded by his son David II (1329–71), a very disturbed time ensued during which the English renewed their attacks; many of the finest abbeys in the south were destroyed and even Holyrood was sacked. Not surprisingly, there was a falling off in new building and in the construction of elaborate tombs for a while. David died childless, and the throne passed to his sister's son by Walter the Steward whose ancestors had come to Scotland in David I's reign and who had built a great abbey at Paisley to the glory of God and to house their tombs. It was natural that Marjorie, the mother of the first of the Stewart kings, should be buried there.

Robert II, 1371–90, was, as a young man, "tall and robust, modest, liberal, gay and courteous . . . generally beloved by true hearted Scotsmen" but by the time he became king he was fifty-four, an ageing man for those times and for the difficulties he had to face, not least of which was the uncertainty as to whether his marriage to his first wife was invalid as a result of their cousinship. He was also too gentle a man for his times, "a tenderer heart no man might have"; "he would not suffer the people to sustain the damage done to them through stamping down their corn by the multitude of people that was at his coronation, but paid the same with large money". And there was the question of the defence of the Border, but here he

23. *A tomb by tradition that of Marjorie Bruce in Paisley Abbey. Not only did misfortune come to her during her long period as a prisoner of the English but shortly after her release in 1316 she suffered a fall from her horse while she was pregnant, and she was killed, though her baby survived. All the earlier heads of the Stewart family were buried here and, incidentally, Robert II, and it would have been natural for his mother too, so this tomb traditionally is hers. But it may have been reconstructed in 1817 from more than one original; the heraldic panels on one side show the arms of Abbot Lithgow, on the other those of Bishop Wishart of Glasgow, but at the foot is the Stewart fess-cheque or draught-board pattern. Over the recumbent lady's head is an impressive and unusual canopy.*

Most of the abbey built by the Stewarts was destroyed by the English at this time; the Decorated architecture that survives—notably the fine west doorway—dates from the fifteenth century.

24. *The tomb of 'The Wolf of Badenoch', Dunkeld Cathedral, Perthshire. Alexander, Earl of Buchan, not the English, was responsible for the destruction of perhaps our finest cathedral, Elgin, in fury at its bishop's resisting his depredations in the north-east; no man ever deserved less to be buried in church. The central figure lies on an altar tomb in full and meticulously carved armour (described in* Proceedings of the Society of the Antiquaries of Scotland, *1958–9, by A. V. Notman). The side panels are not, as often, heraldic but of armed men, which is more appropriate as there was nothing chivalrous about the Wolf.*

A slightly later tomb in Dunkeld is that of Bishop Cardney, c.1436, who not only gave the original glass which used to grace the windows but built the nave up as far as the blind storey. Also of note—in the Chapter House —is a Stewart tomb of the seventeenth century, transitional between Gothic and Renaissance.

was well served by Douglas at Otterburn (see page 83). In 1384 he handed over the government of the country to his eldest son, later Robert III, 1390–1406, but he too was rendered unfit to govern when, four years later, he received a kick from a horse, and power was deputed to the next brother, the Earl of Fife, later Duke of Albany. None of them could control a third brother, Alexander Earl of Buchan and Lord of Badenoch.

As Regent for Robert III, Albany was notorious for his rapacity and insolence, and there was considerable rivalry between him and the heir to the throne, the Duke of Rothesay, a hardly more attractive character. For a time the King transferred power to the latter but Albany managed to create distrust in Robert's mind; Rothesay was arrested and put into the custody of Albany at Falkland Palace where he conveniently died—too conveniently in contemporary opinion. Nor were the times any more settled when Robert himself for a brief time undertook the management of the country. In an attempt to put an end to one of the endemic feuds in the Highlands, he could think of no better way than to arrange for two clans to engage in trial by combat in his presence with thirty chosen champions on either side. This "Battle of the Clans" took place in 1396 on the North Inch (still an open space), Perth, within sight of the Blackfriars' Monastery where the King was staying. Its organization would have been in the hands of the Hereditary High Constable, the Baron of Erroll, head of the family of Hay. This family and that of Keith (who became Hereditary Earls Marshal) had risen to power in the north-east after the decline of the Comyns, the original Earls of Buchan.

The Clan Chattan was one of the contestants; the other has been variously suggested as the Cummins, the Camerons or the Chisholms. Scott in his *Fair Maid of Perth* plumped for Clan Kay.

When Robert III died ("the worst of Kings and the most unhappy of men" as he called himself), his surviving son James I was only twelve years old and, in any case, a prisoner of the King of England; he had been captured by pirates on his way to

France to which his father was sending him for safety from any evil designs that Albany might have. This was a chance for the latter, now again Regent, to try to secure for his family the valuable Earldom of Ross which included much of Inverness-shire and the Isle of Skye. Since it was also wanted by Donald, Lord of the Isles, who had raised a large force to back that claim, a bloody battle ensued at Harlaw, Aberdeenshire, in 1411. Albany's forces were commanded by his nephew, son of "The Wolf", who had made himself Earl of Mar by forcibly abducting the widowed Countess, and who won the day. One of those killed was Sir Gilbert de Greenlaw.

A digression is necessary now to explain how the Lords of the Isles had come to enjoy such an independent position, and also their influence on the art of the West Highlands and especially on funerary monuments.

The Norsemen had been able to establish themselves not only in Shetland and Orkney but also all down the Hebrides and

25, left. The tomb of Sir William Hay of Lochloy in Elgin Cathedral, 1421. Sir William was a cadet of the Hays of Erroll. He lies in plate armour, his head resting on two pillows, his feet apart and resting on an animal of some sort. There are other tombs at Elgin which, though worn, are interesting for their elaborate arches, one of them a very flattened ogee.

26. The tomb of Sir Gilbert de Greenlaw, Kinkell Church, near Inverurie, Aberdeenshire—an incised slab showing the knight in chain mail, very waisted and girt with sword and dirk. The church also has a notable Sacrament House.

into the Isle of Man. These last were ruled from 1115 to 1153 by Olaf, King of Man. When he died, his son-in-law Somerled, half-Scot, half-Norse, fought a great sea battle against Olaf's son Godfrey and by defeating him gained all the southern Hebrides for himself. Somerled's son Dougal received Lorne, Mull, Coll and Tiree, and was the progenitor of the MacDougall Lords of Lorne. Another son Reginald inherited Islay, Kintyre and Ardnamurchan, and *his* son Donald was the progenitor of the MacDonald Lords of the

Isles. They had a divided allegiance—to the King of Scotland for their mainland territory, to the Norwegian King for the Isles; but neither overlord was in any position to exercise any real control over them. During one attempt to bring the MacDonalds to heel, Alexander II of Scotland died on the Island of Kerrera. A King of Norway died in Orkney in 1265 on his return from a similar attempt to demonstrate his strength in which he was defeated by Alexander III. Thereafter, both the MacDonalds and the MacDougalls accepted that the southern Hebrides were part of the domains of the King of Scotland, but that did not put the latter as yet in effective control of those outlying parts.

Within the west, though, there did come a shift in power during the next century, partly as a result of the Wars of Succession. The MacDougalls backed Balliol (being connected by marriage with the Red Comyn) as a result of which they lost Dunstaffnage Castle and much of Lorne to Bruce's supporters, the Campbells. The MacDonalds, too, backed Bruce and received Morven and Mull (which later passed to the Macleans).

The fourteenth century (especially the years 1330-86, when Good John of Islay was Lord of the Isles) has always been looked back to as a Golden Age; under his patronage there grew up in Iona a tradition of monumental carving that is one of the glories of Scotland. He had married, as his second wife, Margaret, daughter of Robert Stewart, then Regent and later King Robert II, but unfortunately friendly relations between the MacDonalds and the Stewarts were not to last. Good John's son, Donald, sought the support of the King of England when he tried to secure the Earldom of Ross (see the Battle of Harlaw, above). And fratricidal feuds with the Macleans, and even with members of their own family, bedevilled the fortunes of later Lords. But at the height of their power they lived in a regal fashion, summoning their subordinate Chiefs to attend their Council; Maclean of Duart, Maclaine of Lochbuie, MacLeod of Harris and MacLeod of Lewis were of the first rank; Mackinnon, Macknaie, MacNeill of Gigha and

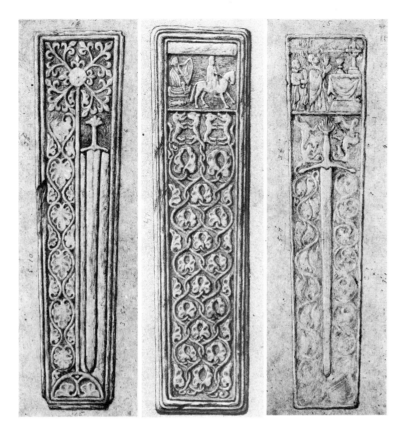

*27 a, b and c. Fourteenth-century grave-slabs in West Highland style,
Iona. Left: This tapered slab is an early example from the Iona school.
The formalized cross with its delicate design and its equally formalized
three-leaved foliage is typical, as is the 'false relief' obtained by first
drawing the design on the flat stone and then cutting away the background
to a depth of about one centimetre. The deceased is unnamed, but his
standing is symbolized by the single-handed sword; the shape of the
pommel and guard suggests an early date. Middle: In later slabs of the Iona
school, the tapering and the cross tend to disappear, and there is often, as in
this case, a panel at the head or the foot showing a boat or small human
figures such as that of this horseman followed by a harpist. The three-
leaved foliage and the intertwined stems are very characteristic. Iona is
particularly rich in such slabs. Right: Here the small picture is of a priest
celebrating Mass, attended by a server. Similar slabs are found in eastern
Scotland but much less delicately carved, as for instance that in Roxburgh
Churchyard, 1371, which commemorates the daughter of a rich merchant,
Robert Balloch. Alongside a floriated cross, it bears a pair of shears.*

28. *Bricius MacKinnon, the Abbey Museum, Iona, fourteenth century.* This is one of the best preserved of all the effigies. On the pillow is a Lombardic inscription stating that the stone commemorates Bricius (who may have been the MacKinnon who is known to have fought at Bannockburn) and his sons Eugenius and Cornebelly. Another commemorates Finguine, the son of Cormac, and Finlag, the son of Finguine, and Eogan—five generations in all. The date makes it possible that the Finguine referred to is the wicked Green Abbot of Iona who "for a long time maintained a certain woman as his concubine, and has had several sons and daughters by her, and has nurtured the said concubine, sons and daughters, out of the goods of the said monastery, and has married three of his daughters with a large dowry from the same goods". The tall helmet or basinet of the knight, the chain mail on the neck and shoulder, and the aketon (an over-garment less protective than mail but much lighter and more suitable for irregular Highland warfare), together with the type of sword, suggest that the effigy was carved some time after Bricius's death —certainly not before the second half of the fourteenth century. Similarly armed figures from the same school may be seen at Iona and at Killean in Kintyre and Kilmory, Knapdale; a considerably later effigy is that at Kilninian in Mull, which has a large two-handed claymore. Kilmartin has some simpler figures from the Loch Awe school and—from much later—a cross of great beauty, with the figure of Christ crucified.

29. *The tomb of Abbot John in Iona Abbey. John, who was Abbot for most of the second half of the fifteenth century, was also a MacKinnon—the illegitimate son of a Chief of that clan, Lachlan, by a noblewoman. The tomb, which shows him in full Mass vestments, was prepared before his death, and the space left for the date in the incised inscription was never filled in.*

MacNeill of Barra, of the second; four more lay kinsmen; the Bishop of the Isles and the Abbot of Iona. Nor was the accession of a Lord of the Isles lacking in pageantry. On an island in Loch Finlaggan, Islay,

> was a big stone of seven feet square, in which there was a deep impression made to receive the feet of MacDonald; for he was crowned King of the Isles standing in this stone, and swore that he would continue his vassals in the possession of their lands and do exact justice to all his subjects; and then his father's sword was put into his hand. The Bishop of Argyll and seven priests anointed him King, in the presence of all the heads of the tribes in the isles and continent, and were his vassals; at which time the orator rehearsed a catalogue of his ancestors.

The end came when the fourth Lord made a treaty with Edward IV of England in 1463 by which he should divide Scotland with the Douglases, for which, when it was discovered, he was forfeited by the King of Scotland; briefly restored, he was finally forfeited in 1493. From that date, though the MacDonald claimants to the Lordship were often a thorn in the flesh of the Stewarts, their great days were over. When, in the seventeenth century, they are found fighting *for* the Stewarts, it is less out of loyalty than to recover some of their lost lands from the Campbells; hence the desertion of Montrose by his MacDonald lieutenant, Colkitto.

From the earliest days of Somerled and his sons, the Lords of the Isles had been patrons of the church; from the days of Good John of Islay, they became patrons of the arts too. Over 600 carved stone monuments from the fourteenth, fifteenth and sixteenth centuries survive to bear witness (and countless more have been lost), the greatest concentration being on the mainland and in the islands of Argyll. They have been examined, described and analysed on behalf of the Royal Commission on the Ancient and Historical Monuments of Scotland by K. A. Steer and J. W. M. Bannerman in *Late Monumental Sculpture in the West Highlands*, a book in which the interest of the artistic criticism and of the history is matched by the beauty of the illustrations. By means of a careful study of the types of rock used and the decorative detail employed by the carvers, together with such inscriptions as have survived, the authors have identified four distinct schools and also the work of a number of independent craftsmen, and have also enabled approximate dating. Apart from the details of the leaves and patterns and shapes, the various types of weapons and armour depicted have helped in the dating—for instance, the two-handed claymore is not thought to have been used in Scotland before about 1500, nor is Black Letter or Gothic, as opposed to the later Lombardic, lettering, which helps for dating the inscriptions. The main source of inspiration for the decoration is Romanesque, but Anglo-Saxon, Viking, and above all Irish, influences have their share. Flat gravestones in low relief, effigies in the round and free-standing crosses were all produced.

To select half a dozen as representative of all is impossible, but my illustrations include two grave-slabs, three effigies—of a man in armour, an ecclesiastic and a lay woman (rare)—a cross, and the unique wall tomb of Alexander MacLeod at

30. Figures from a tomb at Ard-chattan Priory, Argyll. There are six figures in the remains of the Vallis-caulian Priory of Ardchattan near Connel Ferry, Argyll. Here are two successive priors, brothers, of the MacDougall family. Once all-powerful round here, they later lost the priory and its lands to the Campbells. Unlike Abbot John, they are not in magnificent vestments but in their plain outdoor habits. But it is the other figures which are of special interest—a third brother clad in the armour of about 1500, his father in rather more old-fashioned armour, and the sons' mother in a stylish head-dress—there are not many other laywomen por-trayed. A symbol of mortality com-pletes the scene—a corpse with a toad gnawing at its vitals.

31. *A free-standing cross from Kilmory, Knapdale, Argyll. A third type of West Highland memorial was the free-standing cross carved in the same style—no longer the heavy wheel cross of earlier times (see Illustration 10) but more slender, with a solid disc at the centre which sometimes bears a representation of Christ on the Cross. Lovely crosses from the Iona school may be seen on Iona itself (St Martin's Cross), on Islay at Kilchoman, and at Inveraray and Campbeltown. But Iona was not the only source; other schools, less skilled on the whole and less long-lived, have been identified in Kintyre (probably connected with Saddell Abbey) and at Kilmory on Loch Sween and round Loch Awe. This cross from Kilmory has Lombardic lettering which suggests that it is earlier than 1500 and, therefore, the Alexander MacMillan whom it commemorates could be the one who was Keeper of Castle Sween in 1480. On the one side is a rather primitive crucifix with a sword below; on the other, this scene of a huntsman with axe and horn and three hounds attacking a stag. There is a cross of 1516 at Lerags near Oban.*

32, opposite. *The tomb of Prioress Anna Maclean at Iona. Yet another school arose when that of Iona ceased work after the fall of the Lords of the Isles. It was probably founded by a craftsman who went from Iona to the island of Oronsay, to the Augustinian Priory there. This could account for Anna, whose nunnery was also of the Augustinian Order, sending to Oronsay for her tomb. Unfortunately it is broken, but the half which survives is a most lifelike portrait of a stout lady with her two little lapdogs nestling in her robes—enchanting and ˙undoubtedly the most remarkable of the entire West Highland series".*

33. The tomb of Alexander MacLeod, Rodil Church, Harris. Erected in 1528 by Alexander MacLeod of Dunvegan and Harris (d.1547) in the little church of St Clement, Rodil, this wall-tomb is on a larger scale and wholly different from the other West Highland tombs, and the interest lies less in the effigy itself than in the elaborate canopy which surmounts it and in the little low-relief carvings within and on the canopy. The Chief of the MacLeods had always been one of the counsellors of the Lords of the Isles, the furthest and probably the most independent. But this Alexander lived after the fall of the Lordship, which may be the reason why he broke with family tradition and made his tomb in Harris rather than in Iona. Above his effigy are his castle (not thought to be a portrait of Dunvegan as it then was) and his galley, and, between them, the Virgin and Child, flanked by St Clement and another bishop. Beneath is a truly remarkable hunting scene: a long-robed MacLeod with attendants and hounds in pursuit of a very fine stag. A picture of St Michael and Satan at the Day of Judgement completes the inset, while around the canopy are twelve apostles. These are no conventional representations and must, I feel, be regarded as giving some idea of what venerable men looked like in those days, just as the galley gives us an idea of their boats. The stone comes from Mull, but the carving was probably done on the site. Also at Rodil are two other full-size effigies, several slabs and the head of a once free-standing cross.

Rodil in the Island of Harris. For those who are unable to enjoy all the additional pleasures of visiting the west to see the concentration of these monuments in their original setting, there is the book above mentioned; and in the National Museum of Antiquities in Edinburgh there are casts of a grave-slab from Kilmory, Knapdale, with the characteristic border ornament associated with the Loch Awe school of carving and another from Colonsay with the emblematic sword, and hounds savaging a stag.

34. Late medieval slabs, Kilmory, Knapdale, Argyll. A number of interesting slabs have been collected into the chapel at Kilmory. They include good examples of interlacing patterns, large and small effigies, weapons, ships and even tools such as tailors' shears.

35. *The tomb of the fourth Countess of Douglas in Lincluden Abbey, Dumfries. The pedestal is plain with nine shields, but the arch is exceptionally distinguished. Standing on short pillars, it is semicircular, rising to a crocketed finial, the whole framed by slender buttresses and a cornice. The foliage on the mouldings of the arch and on the cornice is elaborate.*

78

FOUR

James I—James IV, 1406–1513

From the age of twelve to the age of twenty-nine—that is to say for the first seventeen years of his reign—James I was a captive in England while first his uncle Albany, and then Albany's son Murdoch, ruled in their own interests; neither saw any attraction in trying to secure the release and return of their lawful King. When, in 1423, James did succeed in obtaining his freedom, he returned to find a land in desperate need of strong government. In the circumstances he may be forgiven for trying to do too much too fast, but he was determined that "if God grant me life, though it be but the life of a dog, there shall be no place where the key shall not keep the castle and the bracken bush the cow". His laws were meant to be far-reaching; the great barons were to be brought to heel; lesser men who could show no useful employment were to be made to work and not to prey on others; wolves were to be hunted down. On the other hand, to ensure the defence of the realm from outside aggression, all able-bodied men were to learn to shoot with the bow (or to wield some other appropriate weapon) and were to parade four times a year to show their arms. Football in particular was not to be allowed to interfere with this more important duty in life. To enforce his peace, the King's Court of Justice was strengthened, though it did not yet have the permanent paid judges with legal expertise that were necessary for it to become an effective instrument of true justice.

36. *The tomb of Sir John Forrester the younger and his wife, Corstorphine c.1450. The elder Sir John Forrester, who was Chamberlain and Master of the Household to James I, lies with his wife under a flattened arch, with his shield and crest above; below are five shields, three bearing his arms and two those of his wives, one a St Clair (or Sinclair) and one a Stewart, c.1444. The tomb shown here is that of his son; the arch is even flatter, but the ornamentation round the heraldry is more elaborate. A third monument is believed to be that of the Chamberlain's grandson. He lies alone and more simply, but his armour is the best preserved. The date of his death is not known, but it was after 1467. In both double tombs, the belts of the knights and the head-dresses of the ladies repay attention.*

Inevitably, James made enemies among those who had found the weak central government an opportunity to enrich themselves. Murdoch and his family were got rid of, to general satisfaction, and the powerful office of Chamberlain which they had monopolized for forty years was given to a lesser man, Sir John Forrester, who, with his son and grandson, are buried in the Collegiate Church of Corstorphine, Edinburgh.

Unfortunately, Sir Robert Graham of Kincardine, who had been arrested with Murdoch, escaped and nursed his resentment in secret while James tried to extend his power even into the Highlands. And, after James insisted on Graham's nephew exchanging the important Earldom of Strathearn for the lesser one of Menteith, he embarked on a plan to kill the King while he was staying in the Blackfriars Monastery for a meeting of the Parliament in Perth. One night early in 1437, he and others were admitted by Sir Robert Stewart, who with his grandfather the Earl of Atholl was privy to the plot. James hid below the floorboards but was pulled out and butchered before his wife's eyes. She did not forgive, and when the plotters were quickly apprehended, they were fearfully tortured before being finally executed.

The Douglases

For her six-year-old son, the fifth Earl of Douglas was at first Regent. He came from the most powerful non-royal family of Scotland, the members of which constantly married Stewart ladies and indeed eventually challenged the Stewart succession. They are the best represented of all in our monuments. Of Norman origin, they succeeded Alan of Galloway in his wide lands of the south-west, and in the stewardship of Kirkcudbright and the Sheriffdom of Wigtown; from their base there, they did sterling service against marauding Englishmen from the time of Sir William le Hardi who joined Wallace in 1297 and eventually died, like him, in the Tower of London. Of his sons Sir James the Good

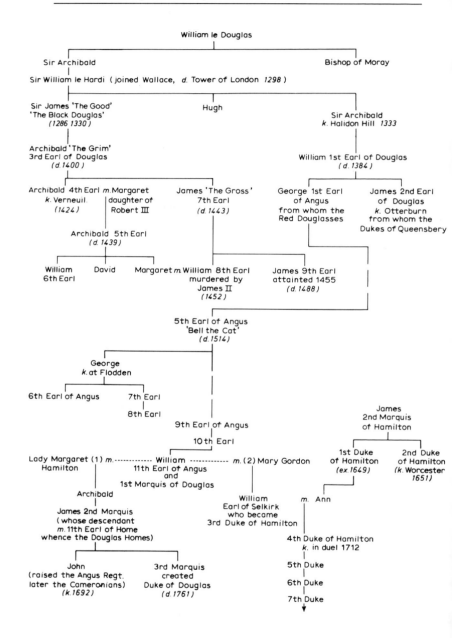

37. *The Douglases.*

was a friend and companion in arms of the Bruce. It was he who was chosen to take the King's heart to the Holy Land on the Crusade which Bruce had vowed but been too preoccupied to undertake. Sir James was the progenitor of the Black Douglases.

From another son, Sir Archibald, were descended the Red Douglases. He was the father of the first Earl of Douglas, and the grandfather of the second, the one killed beating the Percies at the Battle of Otterburn in 1388 and immortalized in "The Ballad of Chevy Chase":

> But I hae dream'd a dreary dream,
> > Beyond the Isle of Skye.
> I saw a dead man win a fight,
> > And I think that man was I.

From him (see the genealogical table), the Earldom of Douglas passed back to an illegitimate son of Sir James the Good— Archibald the Grim who tended to overshadow his king, Robert III. He secured that King's daughter as a wife for his son, who was to be the fourth Earl, the vigorous but unlucky fighter who features in Shakespeare's *Henry IV, Part I*:

> Renowned Douglas whose high deeds,
> Whose hot incursions and great name in arms
> Holds from all soldiers chief majority
> And military title capital
> Through all the kingdoms that acknowledge Christ.

This Earl eventually became Lieutenant General of the French army and Duke of Touraine. The fifth Earl was for a time Regent for James II and was buried in St Bride's Church, Douglas, in 1438, but his mother, who outlived him, chose the Abbey of Lincluden for herself.

When the fifth Earl died, his two sons were quickly caught up in the struggle between Sir Robert Crichton and another of the lesser barons, Sir Alexander Livingstone, for control of the child James II. Differing and distrusting each other on almost all things, they were united in not wanting any interference

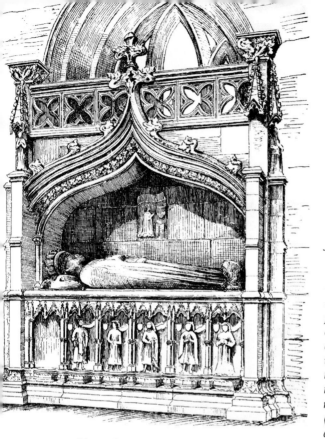

38. The fifth Earl of Douglas, St Bride's Church, Douglas, Lanarkshire. The Earl, who died in 1439, lies in his robes and the coronet of a French duke, with his feet resting on a lion. Six panels adorn the side of the tomb, with small figures probably representing his children. Above is an ogee (or inward-curving) arch and a parapet pierced with quatrefoils. The chapel would be worth visiting for this tomb alone, but there is also the much-worn effigy (from the thirteenth century) of Marjorie Abernethy, wife of Hugh Douglas, the fine tomb of the seventh Earl (Illustration 39) and an alabaster and marble memorial to the eleventh Countess of Home who died in 1877.

39, opposite. The tomb of the seventh Earl of Douglas, d.1443. Although he died only four years after the fifth Earl, and was buried in the same church, his tomb is markedly different; instead of being ogival, and plain underneath, the arch is pointed and flattened and decorated with cusps below and crockets above. (Cusps and crockets used as ornamentation can be seen even more clearly in Illustration 47. The former is the meeting of two curves, the latter a leafy decoration.) Above a more delicate finial than the fifth Earl's are his coat of arms and his crest. Below the two life-size effigies are smaller ones of their six sons and four daughters—no lay figures but each one in his appropriate costume. So too the Countess is particularly splendid in her embroidered robes and fashionable head-dress.

from the Douglases. They invited the sixth Earl and his brother to dine in Edinburgh Castle, of which Crichton was Governor, and there, the story goes, a black bull's head was placed on the board before them to signify their impending fate. Then, after the travesty of a trial in the young King's presence, and in spite of his pleas for mercy for them, the brothers were hurriedly executed in the Castle courtyard:

> Edinburgh Castle, Toune and Towre,
> God grant thou sink for sinne,
> And that e'en for the black dinoir
> Earl Douglas got therein.

The fact that their heir was their great-uncle, James the Gross, and that he made no protest, led men to think that he was a consenting villain. This seventh Earl was also buried at Douglas.

The seventh Earl got the title but not the lands, which went to the sixth Earl's sister, but the eighth Earl remedied this by marrying the lady. He did not enjoy either for long. He made a

40. *The tomb of Lord Borthwick and his wife, St Mungo's Church, Borthwick, Midlothian, where church and castle stand remote, with a really remarkable view. Lord Borthwick was one of those sent as a hostage to England when James II was released in 1424. He built the south transept of the church (which also has a Romanesque apse but is otherwise nineteenth century). Originally the tomb stood in the apse; its distinguishing feature is the exceptional state of preservation of the effigies, which even retain traces of the original colouring, especially on the sword. It is, however, possible that the tomb may be that of Lord Borthwick's son who was at one time employed on a diplomatic mission to the Court of St James. At present the transept is not structurally sound and is closed to the public, but what seems more dangerous is its dampness.*

band with the Earl of Crawford which James II considered a threat. No sooner did the latter come of age than he summoned Douglas (under safe conduct) to his presence in 1452 and, when Douglas refused to renounce the band, murdered him with his own hand in a fit of rage. The Attainder of the ninth Earl in 1455 completed the downfall of the Black Douglases. When, in due course, the family were once again to prove a menace to the monarchy, it was the Red Douglas line, in the person of the fifth Earl of Angus, descended from William the first Earl of Douglas (see Illustration 37).

Later Douglases became Dukes—of Douglas, of Queensberry, of Buccleuch, and even, through marriage, of Hamilton, though for generations there had been much rivalry between Douglases and Hamiltons. Yet another branch married into the Border family of Home and became the ancestors of Sir Alec Douglas-Home, Lord Home of the Hirsel.

For further Douglas memorials see Illustrations 67 and 68. There are also somewhat dilapidated effigies at Dalkeith, the heraldry of which shows them to be of the same family. They are probably late fifteenth century and are interesting because the man—unusually for that date—is in civilian dress. They could be those of James, fourth Lord of Dalkeith, and his wife Joanna, daughter of James I. Other Douglases were buried at Melrose Abbey.

A Borthwick tomb makes an interesting comparison with Douglas tombs.

James II (1437–60)

Douglas, the first Regent during James's minority, soon died and a time of serious disorder followed with the principal contenders for power being the Queen Mother, the Crichtons and the Livingstones. When James did eventually come of age in 1449, he proved quite as vigorous as his father, a better soldier and more popular—though as Professor Donaldson points out, he may have been fortunate in dying young, so far as his reputation is concerned. Had he lived, he might have been corrupted by power and grown more rapacious as other members of his family did. He swept the Livingstones away, and when an attempt to work with the Douglases was evidently failing—they had made a band with the recalcitrant Lords of the Isles and then with the notorious Earl "Beardie" of Crawford—he killed the eighth Earl of Douglas with his own hands, the one grave blot on his reign. To counter these older families which were a danger, he created new Earldoms—of Argyll (Campbell), Marischal (Keith), Morton[1] and Rothes (Leslie), all of which were destined to play very influential parts in Scottish history in the years to come.

Sir Duncan Campbell of Loch Awe, the grandfather of the first Earl of Argyll, founded the Collegiate Church of Kilmun and his mid-fifteenth-century tomb is in the family mausoleum there (not open to the public). According to tradition the alabaster tomb was made in Rome but it bears a strong resemblance to a monument in Northleach church, Oxfordshire, for Sir Ralph de Wilcote and his wife. Sir Duncan lies in plate armour of a somewhat old-fashioned type as worn by the Black Prince (who died in 1376), the head resting on a tilting helmet with his crest of a boar's head. All the details of his equipment down to the superbly ornamented spur straps are almost identical with Sir Ralph's. And Sir Duncan's wife Marjorie, daughter of the Duke of Albany, has the same pearls on her head-dress, and the same jewellery and embroidery, as Lady Wilcote.

It was in James II's reign that magnates took to building Collegiate churches, often with money that came into their hands from those monasteries which were losing their popularity as they failed to keep to their original austerity.

---

[1] James Douglas, first Earl of Morton, and his wife who was a daughter of James I, are buried in St Nicholas Church, Dalkeith, but their effigies are much worn.

41. Sir Duncan Campbell of Loch Awe, Kilmun, Argyll. These are the only effigies at Kilmun, but there is a monument to the eighth Duke of Argyll in Iona Abbey. The eleventh Duke was buried in a resting-place of his forebears, yet older than Kilmun, the island of Inishail on Loch Awe.

Such churches were served by secular priests whose dual function was to maintain the offices of the Church with ceremonial and music not possible in the ordinary parish church, and to say Masses for the souls of the departed, particularly those of the founder and his family. Sometimes they were built new as with Rosslyn, the latest and most ornate of all; at other times a parish church was converted as at Seton. Both are near Edinburgh and should on no account be missed. Rosslyn's architecture is unique, especially the famous Prentice Pillar, but it also has an incised slab of a knight of the fifteenth century, and a small wall tomb of an Earl of Caithness, a descendant of the Sinclair Earl who founded the chapel. Seton Collegiate Church is simpler and covers a longer period of building, but it is no less lovely. The Seton family (later, strong Catholic supporters of Mary Queen of Scots) made it Collegiate in 1493. It was sacked by the English in 1544; then partly rebuilt though the tower was never actually completed. Restored in the nineteenth century by the neighbouring Earl of Wemyss, it is in the custody of the Department of the Environment. The notable and well-preserved tomb within should be that of the founder, the third Lord Seton who died 1478. That lord was in fact buried in the Blackfriars', Edinburgh, but the plate armour depicted is, according to Colin McWilliam's *The Buildings of Scotland, Lothian*, too early for the fourth Lord who died in 1508. The arch above is not unlike that of Lord Borthwick but plainer; the dress of Lady Seton is very similar to that worn by the Lady Collison of Menzies whose effigy is now in the Church of St Nicholas, Aberdeen.[2] Other tombs of the fifteenth century are in Houston Church, Renfrewshire, and in Renfrew itself (Illustration 42). Again a marked similarity has been noticed (*Proceedings of the Society of the Antiquaries of Scotland*, 1893–5). Two others are in Fife (both removed from their original settings) in the churches of Cupar and Ceres. Seton Collegiate Church also contains two characteristic wall monuments without effigies from the seventeenth century. Another parish church which was converted to Collegiate status may be seen at Arbuthnott in Kincardineshire; it houses the tomb of the thirteenth–century Hugo de Arbuthnott.

James II's passion for hunting and for tournaments was thought to be fitting for a king and he also had the gift of getting on with ordinary people; he was "fellow to every private soldier". Fascinated by new things, he imported guns from overseas and did much to build up the royal artillery, which in due course was to strengthen the kings and reduce the power of even their mightiest subjects to hold out against them. Unfortunately his scientific curiosity led to his early

---

[2] St Nicholas, Aberdeen, also contains a sixteenth-century effigy of an Irvine of Drum.

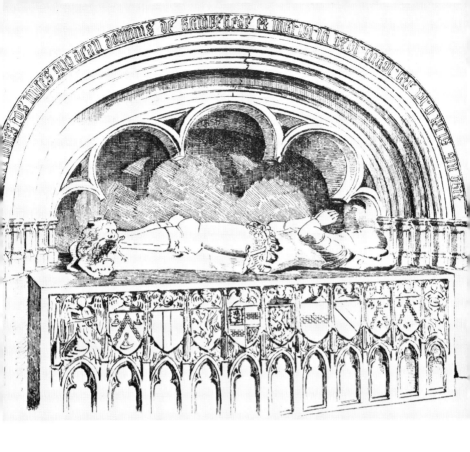

42. *The monument of Sir John Ross and his wife, Renfrew Church, late fifteenth or early sixteenth century.* Rogers, in Scottish Monuments and Tombstones, *says of Sir John that he "attained distinction by overcoming in single combat an English champion sent by his Sovereign to challenge all Scotland. The Englishman was of gigantic stature, while Ross was under middle height. To compensate for his inequality of size, he clothed himself in a dress of skin, the smooth side out, which he rendered slippery with oil. The stratagem succeeded. In struggling with him, the Englishman was unable to retain his grasp, while Ross at length contrived to throw both his antagonist's arms out of joint." This tomb, which originally stood under an arch bearing the following inscription: "Hic jacet Johes: Ros miles quo[n]dam dominus de Hawkehede et Marioria uxor sua: orate pro ipsis qui obit", is now housed in the modern church. Unfortunately, a visitor may arrive at the church to find it locked and with no indication of where to go for access; he will do well to go on to a much more striking modern church at Inchinnan, which has a number of interesting medieval slabs, traditionally those of Templars.*

91

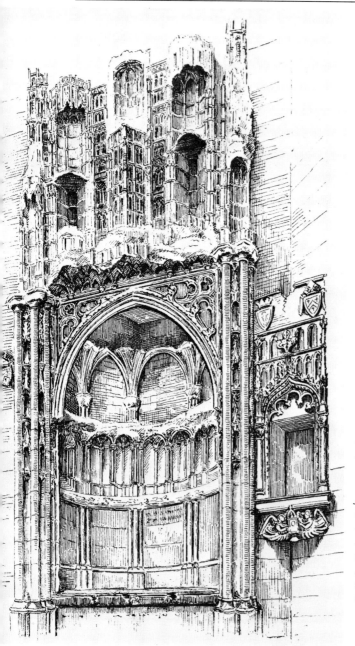

43. *Bishop Kennedy's tomb in the chapel of his St Salvator's College, St Andrews University; very different and, according to Richardson, probably of the school of Tournai in the Netherlands. The arch over the recess is within a square frame, and above is a second storey consisting of an elaborate "house of many mansions", while on each side are two niches to hold statues of saints, now lost. Alongside is an aumbry for the reserved sacrament. Kennedy started his chapel in the same year as he founded the College, 1450.*

death in 1460 when he was killed by a gun exploding during an attempt to recover the Castle of Roxburgh. At first the Royal minority was less disturbed than usual, so long as the King's wise uncle, Bishop Kennedy, survived—but, when he went, the turbulent family of Boyd seized possession of the young King and the peace of the realm was once more disrupted.

James III (1460–88)

At the close of his minority, a marriage was arranged between James and Margaret, daughter of the King of Denmark and Norway, the dowry to be 60,000 florins. When that could not be paid, Orkney was pledged as security for the balance—and then Shetland, too. Orkney was already under the administration of a Scottish earl of the family of St Clair whom James persuaded to exchange these Northern Isles for lands in Fife. It was this earl who started Rosslyn Collegiate Church.

No more than those of his minority were the nineteen years of the King's own rule free from disruption. What have been called his "inexpedient homosexual attachments"—that is, his preference for the company of men such as his tailor and his shoemaker rather than favourites drawn from the noble families—may have offended them less than his preferring the arts to warfare and to hunting. He *did* prefer diplomacy to war and, even more so, poetry, music and old manuscripts to either. Above all he was a builder, and the most unpopular of all his associates, Robert Cochrane, was probably the designer of the Great Hall at Stirling Castle. When finally James overstepped the mark and made Cochrane Master of the Artillery (and possibly Earl of Mar as well), it was the fifth Earl of Angus (now the head of the Douglas family) who volunteered to bell the cat[3] when others were afraid, and the result was the hanging not only of Cochrane but of most of the King's other protégés. Then, when the King replaced the Earl of Argyll as Chancellor with Bishop Elphinstone (an

---

[3] So called from his readiness, when others hesitated, to grasp the nettle and rid Scotland of James III's minions.

admirable appointment) there came a further conspiracy. The Homes, from the Borders, had also been alienated by the King having taken part of the revenues of "their" Priory of Coldingham to endow his Collegiate foundation at Holyrood. The rebels managed to secure the person of, and therefore to claim that they had the approval of, the heir to the throne. James was defeated at Sauchieburn and, after being thrown from his horse, sought help from the miller of Bannockburn, but he was found and murdered, possibly by a priest named Borthwick. All in all, in spite of recent attempts to reappraise it, it was not a glorious reign—and its most conspicuous achievement, the acquisition of the Northern Isles, owed little to James.

James IV (1488–1513)

In every way, the new King found himself in a more secure position than his predecessors. The decline in the fortunes of the Lords of the Isles was completed when the ageing Lord's nephew made an insurrection in the Earldom of Ross, seized Inverness and harried the lands of the MacKenzies who had formerly been dependent on them. They met defeat at the hands of Kenneth MacKenzie of Kintail in 1491 and two years later the Lordship was finally forfeited to the Crown (with which it still rests). It was not the end of trouble in the west but it marks the watershed of the gradual shift of power, there, from the MacDonalds to the Campbells, whose Chief, the Earl of Argyll, was made Lord Lieutenant of the Isles.

   James (the last king to speak Gaelic) felt able to make several progresses in the west by both land and sea, the latter in 1494 and in 1505, with his famous admiral Sir Andrew Wood, though he had a setback on the former occasion when he left behind him a garrison at Dunaverty Castle at the end of the Mull of Kintyre. No sooner had he left, than the MacDonalds hanged his Governor from the walls of the castle. A hundred and fifty years later, they themselves suffered a barbarous massacre on the same spot, inspired by fanatical Puritan ministers.

44. *Kenneth MacKenzie in Beauly Abbey, Inverness-shire. The arch is steeper and plainer, though there is some decoration in the mouldings and on the square crockets above. There were only three Valliscaulian monasteries in Scotland—this, Ardchattan (see Illustration 30) and Pluscarden, now restarted as an active community and being rebuilt. The general design is very like that of a bishop in the ruined cathedral of Fortrose.*

More regularly, the King moved around his Lowlands which enabled him to ensure a greater degree of law and order and a firmer administration of justice than his predecessors had managed. And he further strengthened the Court of Session by adding trained lawyers as professional judges.

His attitude to the Church was somewhat ambivalent. He was devout, he wore day and night an iron belt as a penance for what had happened to his father, he gave money to the poor, he spent on ecclesiastical building, he helped Bishop Elphinstone found the University of Aberdeen, the principal purpose of which was to train men to be priests, but he also thought nothing of diverting Church revenues to maintain his bastard sons and his brother. One of the former was made an archbishop at the age of eleven.

45. *King's College, Aberdeen. The University was founded in 1495 and
the Chapel completed in 1505. It retains its sixteenth-century wooden
carved stalls, the finest in the country. Bishop Elphinstone's altar tomb, which
stands between the pulpit on the left and the episcopal throne on the right, is
quite plain, but an elaborate modern one in bronze stands outside because it
was found to be too large for its original setting. Elphinstone's good work
was carried on by another bishop, Gavin Dunbar, whose tomb is in the
cathedral of Aberdeen, St Machar's. He lies beneath a semicircular arch,
cusped and crocketed, within buttresses and a cornice. The arms are the
Royal Lion Rampant and his own of three cushions. He was the uncle of
Archbishop Gavin Dunbar of Glasgow. In his time the magnificent oak
roof with its painted coats of arms was added. Of the other monuments in St
Machar's, the most striking is a Renaissance tomb dating from Charles II's
revival of Episcopacy, that of Bishop Scougal who died in 1685.*

The University of Aberdeen was the first to have a Faculty of Medicine, which reflects another of James's interests. The Royal Accounts include references to occasions when the King paid people to let him bleed them or extract their teeth. And he founded the Royal College of Surgeons (for its eighteenth-century hall in Edinburgh see Illustration 74).

James too was a great builder, converting the old castles at Falkland and Linlithgow into more comfortable palaces; the former, especially, shows French Renaissance influence, but Gothic continued to predominate in tombs.

He was a lover of the New Learning and helped Chepman and Myllar to set up the first printing press in Scotland. He was the patron of William Dunbar, the poet, who lamented the passing of so many of the makars that James III had also loved:

> (amongst others)
> In Dunfermline (Death) has tane Broun
> With Maister Robert Henrysoun;
> Sir John the Ross embrast has he;
>   Timor mortis conturbat me.
>
> And he has now tane last of a',
> Good gentil Stobo and Quintin Shaw,
> Of quhom all wichtis has pitie;
>   Timor mortis conturbat me.
>
> Good Maister Walter Kennedie
> In point of death lies verilie;
> Great ruth it were that so should be;
>   Timor mortis conturbat me.
>
> Sen he hath all my brether tane.
> He will not let me live alane;
> Of force I man his next prey be;
>   Timor mortis conturbat me.
>
> Since for the death remeid is none,
> Best is that we for death dispone
> After our death that we may live;
>   Timor mortis conturbat me.

Dunbar also wrote "The Thistle and the Rose" for James's marriage to Henry VIII's daughter Margaret Tudor—a sad occasion for the King who would have preferred to marry his mistress, Margaret Drummond. But those who were opposed to the marriage (either for diplomatic or for family reasons) had poisoned her and her two sisters the year before. Three plain slabs in Dunblane Cathedral mark the place of their burial.[4]

Though he was a much more military character than his father, and would have liked to go on a Crusade, and paid much attention to naval matters, he did, so long as he could, remain at peace without loss of territory or honour, a course made easier by the peaceful policies of Henry VII. That ended when Henry died and Henry VIII not only embarked on a war with France, but claimed that he was "the verie owner of Scotland". James felt bound to adhere to the Auld Alliance and led an army of 20,000 men into Northumberland. It was as large as that of his opponent, the Earl of Surrey, but his philosophy did not make him a good general. A foreign visitor said of him: "He is courageous, even more than a King should be . . . he does not take the least care of himself . . . he is not a good captain because he begins to fight before he has given his orders. He does not think it right to begin any warlike undertaking without himself being the first in danger." Though he chose a strong position to withstand any attack at Flodden in 1513 he allowed himself to be drawn from it. His guns were not well manned. The great phalanx of spears, which so long as it kept moving should have proved irresistible, was brought to a halt, and was then outfought by the English bills (which had hacking power as well as thrusting). The King died at their head and with him two bishops (including his son), nine earls, three Highland chiefs, fourteen other lords and countless lesser men—the Flowers of the Forest—though, to be

---

[4] Also in the cathedral is an early, but much worn, effigy of an Earl of Strathearn, of around 1271, with his wife.

honest, the story was rather different from that told in that eighteenth-century ballad, and from that sung in Scott's *Marmion*.

James II's monument at Holyrood has gone, and so has James III's at Cambuskenneth, but James IV never had one—perhaps never even had Christian burial. His body was taken to England where Henry VIII planned to give it a Royal funeral in Old St Paul's but his mind turned to other things; the corpse lay in its coffin, unburied, for many years and its ultimate fate is unknown.

One of those killed was Lord Sempill who was buried at Castle Semple, Renfrewshire.

Four hundred years after the battle, an equestrian statue was set up at Selkirk, but a more living memorial takes place each year there at the Common Riding. The story goes that of eighty Selkirk men who went to the battle, only one returned, one of five Fletcher brothers (or according to another tradition, the leader of the party, William Brydon); he stopped on reaching the market place, and there waved a blood-stained banner that he had captured from the English. To this day, his representative does the same after he has carried the burgh's banner on horseback round the burgh lands. Hawick too has its Common Riding ceremony, and a rather similar statue—to the young men who fought at Horeshole Bridge after their seniors had been killed at Flodden.

46. Monument to Lord Sempill, Castle Semple, Renfrewshire. MacGibbon and Ross say of it that it "shows the last expiring effort of the Gothic spirit. The cusped half-arch, half-lintel is a kind of compromise between the Gothic and the Renaissance, and the exuberant foliage of the upper part shows Gothic forces run wild." In fact, there is surely more that is Gothic than Renaissance here. And there is certainly more Gothic to come.

47. *The Ogilvie tomb at Cullen, Banffshire. Flanking pillars culminate in octagonal pinnacles, as does the finial of the ogee arch over the effigies of the knight and his lady; these are carved in low relief, both kneeling; he is in armour both here and in the main effigy below. Eight small figures on the*

FIVE

James V—James VI, 1513–1625

James V 1513–42

This century, during which the Tudors made themselves so powerful in England, saw further minorities in Scotland—those of James V from 1513–28, of Mary from 1542–60 and of James VI from 1567–83—forty-nine years out of seventy. They saw too the coming of the Reformation, beginning with the burning of George Wishart and (in revenge) the murder of Cardinal Beaton in 1546. Its climax came with the return of John Knox to his native land in 1559. Up till the time of the Reformation, the building of sumptuous tombs and Collegiate churches went on hand in hand, but from then on a decline set in. One of the latest of the purely Gothic memorials is that to Alexander Ogilvie who died in 1554, different and magnificent rather than beautiful.

During James V's minority, the Douglases were as usual to the fore under the sixth Earl of Angus with, as their rivals, the Hamiltons led by the Earl of Arran who could claim a rather closer relationship to the Crown. But there was, in France, an even closer royal relation—Albany, son of James

pedestal, in hoods and long robes, complete the design. Also to be seen in this church are a monument to Chancellor Seafield, one of the architects of the 1707 Union, a fine loft and a Sacrament House, though not quite such an elaborate one as that in the neighbouring church at Deskford.

III's trouble-making brother. Though completely French by upbringing, Albany was recalled to act as Regent and, on the whole, ruled well, though naturally enough with a strong French bias. The result was that Angus looked for support to those who preferred an English alliance. At first it seemed as though Angus might be the stronger, especially when he married the Queen Mother who had possession of the young King; but not for long. Not only did Queen Margaret lose control of the King to Albany; she quickly also tired of Angus who therefore had to wait for his chance till 1524, by which time Albany had returned to France. When he did eventually get control of James, he pandered to all the latter's lowest instincts in the hope of postponing as long as possible his wanting to exercise the royal power for himself. During all this time, good government was in abeyance, and all that Angus really achieved was to make the King thoroughly implacable against the entire Douglas family.

The only redeeming feature of James V's upbringing was that he had, as tutors at different times, two of the outstanding men of the time—first, Sir David Lindsay of the Mount, and then Gavin Dunbar, later to be Archbishop of Glasgow and a very able Chancellor and head of the Court of Session. The former's lines are much quoted:

> How, as ane chapman bears his pack,
> I bore thy Grace upon my back
> And sum tymes, stridlings on my neck,
> Dansand with mony bend and beck.
> The first syllabis that thou did mute
> Was Pa, Da Lyn. Upon the lute
> Then playit I twenty springs, perqueir,
> Whilk was gret piete for to hear.

When James himself did grasp control, he showed a certain early vigour, but was also vindictive, extortionate, ruthless and cruel. The Douglases especially felt his heavy hand, Angus's sister, Lady Glamis, being the most famous victim. It is possible that she may have murdered her husband but she was acquitted of that and it is extremely unlikely that she was really guilty of "treasonably conspiring and imagining the King's slaughter or destruction by poison" but she was burnt alive.

Knox said of him:

> He was called by some a good poor man's King; of others he was termed a murderer of the nobility, and one that had decreed their whole destruction. Some praised him for the repressing of theft and oppression; others dispraised him for the defouling of men's wives and virgins. And yet none spoke altogether beside the truth; for a part of all these foresaid were so manifest that as the virtues could not be denied, so could not the vices by any craft be cloaked.

His popularity with the poor sprang from his liking for going about the country disguised as the "Gudeman of Ballangeich". Many tales have survived, mostly following a set pattern. The King is given hospitality in a poor man's cottage. His host says that he has never even seen the King. "Go to Stirling," or wherever the Court happened to be, says the Gudeman. "But how will I know which is the King?" asks the poor man. "He will be the only one wearing a hat." In due course the poor man does go to Court and is at first confused, and then comforted, by the King. Other tales tell of his amorous adventures and of his encounters with the gipsies, for whom he seems to have had a special fondness.

As long as Gavin Dunbar was his Chancellor, James could count on the backing of the Church, though his attitude to it in return was even more dubious than his father's. He was outwardly pious and he assented to the burning of a number of heretics who leant towards the new doctrines, but he also patronized a severe critic of the Church in the person of his friend, Lyndsay of the Mount, and enjoyed the latter's play *Ane Satire of the Three Estates* in which both clergy and monks were very harshly criticized.

Towards the end of James's reign, he was more influenced by Cardinal Beaton, who was a much less edifying character than Dunbar; he also began to reap the reward of some of his ruthless actions at the start of his personal government when he was trying to instil order into the Borders. And, on the international front, he found that he could no longer play off England against France to maintain peace. Forced to choose between them, he married the daughter of the King of France and, when she died on reaching Scotland, he turned again to France for his second wife and married Mary of Guise. It was an ill-starred match for Scotland. The two sons she bore him both died in infancy, and three more disasters befell him. An army which he raised to fight the English refused to fight; a second was beaten at Solway Moss; his third child proved to be a lass. Already a sick man, he turned his face to the wall and died. His own tomb has not survived but that of one of his friends has, with whom he loved to stay. Lord Somervell is buried with his wife in a small Perpendicular aisle which is all that remains of a Collegiate church at Carnwath, Lanarkshire, of around 1550. She was a daughter of Maitland of Lethington; he had been taken prisoner at Solway Moss. Sadly the effigies on this altar tomb are much decayed.

Mary Queen of Scots 1542–67

Mary's minority, even more than her brief reign while she was in Scotland herself, laid down the lines on which the country's future was to develop. Up till that time, from the victory at Bannockburn to the defeats at Flodden and Solway Moss, the danger to national independence had been England. Now it was from a Queen Mother who was French; her troops were French and the infant Queen was being brought up in France as a Frenchwoman and, in due course, was married to the heir to the French King. There was little reason to suppose that they or their heir, if they had one, would rule both lands from Edinburgh. In fact her royal husband died young and she returned in 1561 to the land of her birth a widow of nineteen, beautiful and with an immense capacity to charm.

It was a very different land from the one she had left. The

reformers burned by her father had not died in vain. First Lutheran and then Calvinist doctrines spread fast and nowhere were the abuses that they attacked worse than in Scotland—the ignorance of so many of the clergy, the pluralism and absenteeism, their neglect of their vows of chastity. In their most extreme form, all these faults were embodied in Cardinal Beaton, Archbishop of St Andrews, ally of the Queen Mother. Those whose interests in reform were theological were joined by others who coveted church lands and who saw how laymen had profited by the Reformation in England. When the saintly George Wishart was burnt, a group of desperate men, including two Leslies and Kirkcaldy of the Grange, in 1546 broke into the Castle of St Andrews where Cardinal Beaton "had been busy at his accounts with Mistress Marion Ogilvy that night who was observed to depart from him by the privy postern that morning; and, therefore, quietness after the rules of physic, and a morning sleep, was necessary for my Lord". The Cardinal pleaded for his life but got no more sympathy than he had shown to Wishart. The body was hung over the Castle walls for all to see and, adds Knox:

> These things we write merrily because the weather was hot (for it was May as ye have heard) and his funeral could not hurriedly be prepared, it was thought best, to keep him from stinking, to give him salt enough, a cope of lead, and a nook in the bottom of the Sea-Tower (a place where many of God's children had been imprisoned before) to await what exequies his bretheren the Bishops would prepare for him.

The upshot was a siege of the murderers in the Castle where, in due course, they were joined by Knox himself who, though he believed that the murder itself was justified, did not approve of the way in which some of the defenders would issue forth to plunder the surrounding countryside, killing and burning, and "using their bodies in lechery with fair women, serving their appetite as they thought good". An elaborate mine was

tunnelled towards the castle walls to be met with a counter-
mine, both of which survive and can be followed to this day,
but the defenders managed to hold out until a French force
arrived with naval support and artillery which they managed
to haul up to the towers of the Cathedral and St Salvator's
College. Such gaps were made in the Castle walls that
Kirkcaldy of the Grange was sent to ask for terms. Knox says
that the commander of the French troops agreed to spare the
lives of the defenders and to transport them to France where
they would be free to enter the service of the King of France or

48. Statue of John Knox, New College, Edinburgh. Knox was buried in the graveyard of St Giles, of which church he had been minister—near where the statue of Charles II now stands. To the modern mind, he is to be respected for his courage and his achievements, rather than loved for his personality, but he did in his lifetime manage to win the love of many of those who knew him most intimately. They did not include Mary, Queen of Scots, whom he reduced to tears on more than one occasion, nor the tougher Elizabeth, who resented his suggestion in his First Blast of the Trumpet against the Monstrous Regiment of Women *that they were weak, frail, impatient and foolish; that they were the port and gate of Hell; and that men were less than beasts to permit such an infringement of God's order as letting them bear rule over them.*

There are, of course, many Knox monuments, the most widely known being the picturesque house in Edinburgh's High Street which, in spite of a sturdy defence reported in Proceedings of the Society of the Antiquaries of Scotland *in the mid-nineteenth century, could not have been his. For all that, it is worth visiting, to invoke the sort of surroundings in which he lived. The nineteenth-century statue illustrated is by John Hutchison in the courtyard of New College, Edinburgh; not far away stands another by Pittendrigh MacGillivray which was moved from inside St Giles to its present position, outside, near his burial place. A slightly earlier memorial of 1825 surmounts the hill of the Necropolis of Glasgow and is accompanied by a long description detailing many of the others who supported the Reformation in its early days. Thomas Chalmers (Illustration 90) preached the sermon at the laying of its foundation stone.*

to go to any country they wanted to, other than Scotland. This is disputed. At any rate, on arrival in France, the gentry were imprisoned in various castles, and the lesser folk including Knox were made slaves in the French galleys for over a year.

When he was eventually freed, he found refuge, first in the England of Edward VI, and then in Calvin's Geneva. Returning to Scotland in 1559, he immediately challenged Mary of Guise's attempts to suppress the fast-growing Protestantism. An inflammatory sermon preached in St John's Kirk, Perth, led to an outbreak of iconoclasm. French troops were called in once more to oppose the Protestant lords but they did not prevail, for Elizabeth of England willed otherwise. So, when the young Queen Mary Stewart returned to Scotland she had no foreigners to enforce her wishes as to the Catholic religion in which she had been brought up and to which she genuinely adhered. In any case, she was no Mary Tudor and she was not married to the King of Spain. As it was, she tried to avoid religious confrontation until much later on when, as a prisoner in England, her only hope of rescue lay in help from one or other of the two great Catholic monarchs.

To start with, she showed herself ready to work with her half-brother Lord James Stewart whom she created Earl of Moray, and William Maitland of Lethington, both among the more moderate Reformers; and she even bore with the irritations of Knox's efforts to convert her—until she could achieve a marriage which might strengthen her position. Disastrously her choice fell on her cousin Darnley with whom she was briefly in love. He had no merits either as a husband or as a politician. He neglected his wife and then, when she turned for help to her Italian secretary, Rizzio, he organized his assassination almost before her eyes. Darnley, in his turn, was murdered by a group thought to have included the Earl of Bothwell so that Mary's subsequent marriage to Bothwell made it appear that she must have had prior knowledge of the plot. She was made a prisoner in the Castle of Loch Leven, and Moray became Regent. (The Douglases were, as ever, near the heart of affairs; the castle was presided over by the Lady Margaret Douglas and, as readers of Scott's *The Abbot* will remember, it was a Douglas who aided Mary's escape by securing the keys of the castle. Incidentally, the Lady Margaret had been, before her marriage, one of the favoured mistresses of James V and was the mother of the Earl of Moray who she felt should have been King in Mary's place.)

Mary's conduct had scandalized Scotland but there was still a strong feeling that an anointed sovereign had a special sanctity, and many were far from happy about deposing her. When she escaped from Loch Leven, she attracted the support

49. *Brass tablet from the tomb of Regent James Stewart, Earl of Moray, St Giles, Edinburgh. The Regent was buried in St Giles on Sunday, 14 February 1570 after a sermon from John Knox, and, above the vault in which he was interred, an altar tomb carried this Latin inscription by George Buchanan. The tomb fell into disrepair when the South Aisle did, but the plate was saved by the family and was replaced when the tomb was reconstructed in the mid-nineteenth century. It is one of the few surviving Scottish Brasses.*

of the Bishops, the Hamiltons and a number of other lords and some 5,000 men. But at Langside, in May 1568, Moray's forces were the stronger and the better led and Mary had to flee the country, wrongly choosing England as a refuge rather than France or Spain, either of which might have been more ready than Elizabeth to take up her cause. That she did so was to the benefit of Scotland in the long run but there was tragedy in the fact that, as Professor Donaldson points out, if it had not been for her disastrous marriage to Darnley, she might have had a long and successful reign, secure in the hearts of her subjects.[1]

[1] Queen Mary's House in Jedburgh, where she nearly died after her long ride to visit Bothwell in 1566, is preserved as a museum of her things.

While in Loch Leven, she had miscarried of twins by Bothwell, conceived before her marriage, and so her only issue was James VI, on whose behalf Moray was Regent. But Moray was murdered in February 1570, and his successors, Lennox and Mar, also died within a year of taking office. James Douglas, fourth Earl of Morton, was more fortunate and ruled wisely and firmly until 1580 when he too fell a victim to faction. Meanwhile, the young King was being given a grim grounding in Calvinist theology by George Buchanan and, fatherless and motherless, was growing up without anyone to love him or anyone to love, the fruits of which may be seen in his subsequent character. Only briefly, between 1579 and 1582, did he find in a rather older cousin, Esmé Stewart, from France, someone whom he could really feel affection for, but that relationship was ended all too soon as a result of the jealousy of certain lords and of the extreme leaders of the Presbyterian party. The King was kidnapped in the "Ruthven Raid" and made to banish Esmé. Eventually a compromise administration evolved, headed by John Maitland of Thirlestane who did much to train James in the arts of statesmanship; then from Maitland's death in 1595, James was truly his own master. And under him Scotland enjoyed peace, the Borders in particular as never before.

James VI 1567–1625

James grew up a strange creature—Calvinist in doctrinal beliefs yet a firm believer in bishops as instruments of Royal policy—capable of ruthlessness yet ever nervous of possible attacks on his person—and, though far-seeing in many of his political aims, blindly indulgent to his favourites. His overwhelming ambition was to obtain the English Crown, and once he had achieved that, he moved south and, in spite of many promises to the contrary, never again lived in Scotland; indeed he made only one visit in twenty years. Those who had political aspirations had to do the same—and others too found

50. George Heriot's School, Edinburgh. "Jingling Geordie" is buried in Greyfriars' Churchyard, but his true monument is this, perhaps the finest of all Renaissance buildings in Scotland. Modelled as an institution on Christ's Hospital, London, construction was begun in 1628 but then delayed by Cromwell who used it as a military hospital; it did not admit its first thirty boys until 1659. In a niche in the courtyard is a likeness of the Founder; he also has a bust over the entrance to the Heriot Watt University building in Chambers Street, Edinburgh.

it profitable, such as George Heriot, the Edinburgh goldsmith who lent large sums to James.

With the King absent, the initiative in the patronage of the arts passed from the Crown to its wealthier subjects, and in many cases these are private grandees rather than the holders of the high offices of state—to which James appointed, if he could, men whom he was better able to influence. Now, after the intermission of the Reformation, there is an almost complete break in style. It coincides nicely with the change of century though there is a fully Renaissance monument of the Lumsden family dated 1598 in the churchyard of Crail. A transitional monument which may be seen at Tarves, Aberdeenshire, is dated 1589—"one of the most remarkable things

111

51. *The tomb of William Forbes of Tolquhon, Tarves, Aberdeenshire, 1589.*

52, opposite. *The tomb of Sir Robert MacLellan of Bombie c.1600, Kirkcudbright. MacLellan was a local magnate and Provost of Kirkcudbright. This tomb is in a small aisle adjoining the house which he built for himself. The semicircular arch above the effigy with its dog-tooth mouldings could have come from a Gothic tomb, but in overall effect the monument is purely classical—the pillars on either side, the cornice, the triangular pinnacles each with a ball on top, the curved console-like ornamentation and the cherub on top. Behind the figure in the arch is a Memento Mori; above, in the spandrels, are portraits of the laird and his wife, recalling the Cullen tomb, and at the very top a cherub above the MacLellan arms, with a ship, the seal of the burgh and the Maxwell motto, "Think on".*

DOMINVS SITVS EST T M LELLANVS ET VXOR
D GRISSEL MAXVELL MARMOR VTRAMOVE TEGIT
HIS GENITVS R D KIRKCVDBRIVS ECCE SEPVLCHRVM
POSVIT HOC CHARI PATRIS HONORE SVI
ILLE OBIT ANNO DOM   1597

of its kind in the North of Scotland", according to W. Douglas Simpson (*Proceedings of the Society of the Antiquaries of Scotland,* 1945–6) "particularly in view of its importance in the history of the spread of Renaissance influence on Scottish architecture during the reign of James VI". Though the general design is traditional—a recess within a cusped semicircular arch—and probably based on Bishop Gavin Dunbar's tomb in St Machar's Cathedral, Aberdeen, the balusters fronting the tomb chest below, and the elaborately carved pillars supporting the cornice, are essentially Renaissance. And the recess is for an inscribed stone rather than for an effigy. Instead, the builder of the tomb, William Forbes of Tolquhon, is depicted on one of the side pillars wearing a ruff and slashed doublet with his wife, equally gorgeously dressed, on the other.

The Menzies memorial has no effigy, though the recess is large enough to contain one. But effigies were out of fashion as a result of the Reformation and the characteristic wall monument of these years was something much smaller, and with a shallower recess, containing an inscription or occasionally a coat of arms, as for instance in a number of late sixteenth-century such tombs in Greyfriars' Burial ground, Edinburgh. Another change is that when, as in a few of the grandest tombs, there *is* an effigy, the deceased is usually shown kneeling or standing, rather than recumbent—perhaps, according to Professor Donaldson, for fear that a figure in the

53. *The Menzies memorial at Weem, Perthshire, 1616. Sir Alexander Menzies was also a local rather than a national figure. What makes his memorial so different—indeed unique—is its dedication to his two wives, his mother, his grandmother, great-grandmother and great-great-grandmother. Here not even the arch is Gothic, and there is no effigy, but there are beautifully carved figures on either side, representing Faith (with a book in her hand) and Charity with a child in her arms and another at her feet. Above the cornice are further, smaller statues; two are kneeling, two are cherubs, and the one on top, with its outstretched arms, represents the all-embracing love of God.*

posture of death might be thought to be encouraging the idea of prayers for a departed soul. The same fear might also account for the virtual concealment of the effigies altogether in the most unusual sepulchre of Thomas Crawford and his wife at Kilbirnie, Ayrshire, of around 1594. It has also been suggested that some of the memorials of this period show Danish influence as a result of James VI's marriage to Anne, daughter of the King of Denmark, and English influence after the Union of the Crowns.

One of the statesmen on whom James most relied was George Home, Earl of Dunbar, who died in England but was brought back for burial in 1611. He had been Lord High Treasurer and an active agent in James's successful keeping of the peace in Scotland, and also in his reintroduction of a modified episcopacy.

Another tomb of very similar design may be seen at Scone Palace, Perth; that of another of James's servants, David Murray, first Viscount Stormont. Professor Donaldson has drawn attention to the very close parallels, not only in the careers of these two men but even in the design of their tombs, in spite of the fact that the Scone tomb is twenty years later than that at Dunbar.

James himself, like all subsequent monarchs, was buried outside Scotland, and there is no contemporary monument of him (to my knowledge) in Scotland. The nearest might be said to be the King James VI Hospital, Perth, but the building which stands today, pleasing though it is, dates from the eighteenth century. But it is interesting in that it stands on the site of the Pre-Reformation Charterhouse where James I was buried after his murder.

---

54. The tomb of George, Earl of Dunbar, in Dunbar Parish Church. Here there is an effigy of Home in his Garter robes. He kneels beneath a classical arch, only the figures in armour on either side recalling more disturbed days, and they are counterbalanced by Justice and Peace in the spandrels above. Black, brown and white marble give warmth to this magnificent composition which Colin McWilliam reckons is English work.

55. *This statue of James VI at Glamis Castle dates from 1686 according to a contract between the Earl of Strathmore and Arnold Quellin, a Dutch immigrant sculptor then working in London (as Dr M. R. Apted has told me). There were originally statues of all four Stewart Kings of the United Kingdoms, but only this and the one of Charles I survive.*

The Union of the Crowns of Scotland, England, Ireland and (the as yet claimed) France is commemorated in a completely different way in the layout of the garden created at this time by Sir David Lindsay at Edzell, Angus. The little box hedges are meticulously clipped into the shape of the emblems of those four countries, while others round the roses in the centre spell out the Lindsay motto "*Dum spiro, spero*".

James may not have been a particularly likeable personality but, all in all, his achievement in Scotland was a notable one. As Professor Donaldson has pointed out:

In choosing his servants, James VI looked for adminis-

56. Edzell Castle and sixteenth-century garden. The garden is open to the public and is surrounded with some notable German sculpture of the same date. To appreciate the garden to the full, it must be looked at not only at ground level but also from the first floor of the comfortable mansion which Lindsay added to an earlier tower house.

trative capacity and loyalty to himself, and he thought that he was more likely to find those qualities in men drawn from the middle class or the younger sons of peers rather than in the holders of ancient peerages. The latter, he felt, would not so easily acknowledge him as their master. At one point he explained in so many words that he did not want to employ great men in his government, but such as he could correct and were hangable . . . none of whom I hasten to say did he hang. Of course some of them became peers, by creations which were the reward of their services. But that is only one link among them. It is indeed striking to find among them both Dunbar the Treasurer and Scone the Comptroller. Then John Maitland of Thirlestane [Illustration 58] was Secretary of State—and Secretary of State in succession to Robert Pitcairn. . . . But Thirlestane besides being Secretary became Chancellor. And Thirlestane's son, the first Earl of Lauderdale, married a daughter of the Earl of Dunfermline, another of James's Chancellors, so that he was both the son and the son-in-law of a Chancellor. And the Earl of Kinnoull, whose monument we saw at Perth [Illustration 57], became Chancellor in succession to Dunfermline. One begins to see what a close-knit group they formed. There are other links too. We have the effigy of John Maitland of Thirlestane, who was with those who held the Castle of Edinburgh for Queen Mary; we have the tomb of Thomas Crawford of Jordanhill, who received the surrender of that castle when Maitland and his friends gave it up. Sir George Bruce of Carnock [Illustration 69], though himself primarily an industrialist, was the brother of Lord Kinross, another of James's hangable men.

However, the lesson of monuments is only by inference a lesson on the government of Jacobean Scotland. It was the period of the painted ceilings, it was the period of the tower-house in its last phase of refinement and sophistication, it was the period of the appearance of completely domestic residences, with no pretence at fortification—a tribute to the peace which King James's servants were enforcing—it was the period of poets like Drummond of Hawthornden and Sir William Alexander, it was the period when Timothy Pont was mapping Scotland and when John Napier[2] was inventing logarithms. I see those remarkable monuments as further proof of the cultivated tastes of a period which I regard as marking one of the peaks of Scottish culture.

[2] John Napier was born at Merchiston Castle in 1550—before his father's sixteenth birthday. Not only did he invent logarithms but also a calculating machine and an improved cannon, and was interested in agriculture and theology. He is commemorated in a nineteenth-century Latin inscription in St Cuthbert's Church, Edinburgh, but was buried in St Giles.

57. *The tomb of the Earl of Kinnoull, Kinnoull Church, Perth, 1635. A*
fully developed Renaissance tomb dismissed by MacGibbon and Ross as
pompous, but it is not without interest for its elaborate ornamentation and for
its division into two compartments. In one, the Earl is standing; in the other
is the bag in which the Chancellor kept the Great Seal. On either side are
pseudo-Corinthian pillars very different from the flat pilasters of the early
post-Reformation wall monuments, and also from the plain round ones of the
Lauderdale and Dunbar tombs. This increasing elaboration is carried even
further by the third Duke of Hamilton's monument from the end of the
seventeenth century (Illustration 67).

58. *The Lauderdale Memorial, Haddington Church, East Lothian. This tomb is not normally visible as the little chapel in which it stands has to be kept locked. It is far more dignified than Kinnoull's and, after a recent refurbishing, glows with colour to give an impression of what so many of these monuments must once have looked like. The effigies are recumbent*

SIX

The Civil Wars of the Seventeenth Century

The seventeenth century saw a complicated interaction of religious, economic and political factors. James VI had been ready, to some extent at least, to temporize. Charles I was not; he was inflexible, ill-informed, and determined to put his Episcopalianism above all other considerations. His policy of trying to enhance the ecclesiastical power of the Bishops, and even to appoint them once more to key positions of secular importance; of reintroducing Arminian theology and ritual; and of recovering, for them, church lands which had been alienated to laymen; none of these had any hope of success. Furthermore, for eight years, Charles did not even pay a visit to the land which he had left as an infant; and when he did come, for his coronation, he gave offence on every hand. He demanded that the Chancellor of Scotland, Hay, Earl of Kinnoull, should yield precedence to the Archbishop of Canterbury, and, when Kinnoull refused, angrily remarked

and of alabaster; the marble glows almost as brightly as the paint. Among the many coats of arms of families with which the Maitlands intermarried are those of the Douglases, Hamiltons, Lindsays, Setons and Drummonds.

The beautiful church is also worth visiting, and its graveyard, which runs picturesquely down to the river, has many interesting table tombs from the seventeenth and eighteenth centuries.

that he would not "meddle further with that cankered, gouty old man".

The monument to an earlier Chancellor, John Maitland, Lord Thirlestane, and to his son the first Earl of Lauderdale, and their wives, is of about the same age as the Kinnoull monument. Thirlestane was the brother of Secretary Maitland and joined him against the Earl of Morton, being lucky to escape with his life after the capitulation of Edinburgh in 1573. He later became James's trusted Chancellor until his death in 1595. His son, who may have erected this monument, was less prominent in public affairs. On the other hand *his* son (who alternatively may have been the builder) was Charles II's chief minister in Scotland and the only Duke of Lauderdale.

After his coronation, Charles I next attempted to force the use of a set Book of Common Prayer on the Scots. Jenny Geddes's famous protest was by no means the only one, and the Bishop of Brechin, when he used the service, thought it wise to lay two loaded pistols on the cushion in front of him. The two Bishops' Wars ensued and led to the summoning of England's Long Parliament and in due course to the outbreak of the Civil Wars. In Scotland, the National Covenant was signed enthusiastically, even by many who, with Montrose, subsequently fought for the King.

There was a short time in 1644–5 when it seemed as though Scotland, at any rate, lay at the feet of the King as a result of the heroic marches of Montrose but in the long run the greater wiles of his rival, the Marquess of Argyll, prevailed and Montrose went to the scaffold to be hanged (as a greater humiliation than being beheaded by the "Maiden". (This precursor of the guillotine survives and may be seen in the National Museum of Antiquities in Edinburgh.) Montrose is a cult figure to this day, and rightly so. To have kept at bay with the small and undisciplined, untrained and constantly changing, forces at his command, the armies marshalled against him—winning tactical victory after victory—demonstrates not only military skill of the highest order but an extra-ordinary personality. He was young and clever and rich and

59. *Moray House in the Royal Mile, Edinburgh. Montrose's monument in St Giles bears a contemporary sword which may have been his, but the tomb is Victorian. Instead here is the window of Moray House from which Argyll (at his son's wedding) is said to have looked down in triumph as his rival went to meet his end on the scaffold.*

beautiful and, if he was also vain and at times arrogant—he would brook no rival—his faults did not diminish the adoration which his men gave to one who not only shared all their hardships but gave them, for a year, glory and success beyond what might seem possible. His politics clashed with his religion; he was a true Presbyterian yet he felt that not only did his first loyalty lie to his King, but that a strong King, even if he were an Episcopalian, was preferable to a state of anarchy "where every man oppresseth his neighbour without any hope of redress from a King despoiled of his power to punish oppressors". His sense of duty clashed too with his love for his wife:

> My dear and only wife, I pray,
> That little world of thee

Be governed by no other sway
Than purest monarchy
For if confusion have a part
Which virtuous souls abhor,
And hold a synod in thy heart,
I'll never love thee more.

Like Alexander, I will reign,
And I will reign alone;
My thoughts did ever more disdain
A rival on my throne.
He either fears his fate too much,
Or his deserts are small,
That dares not put it to the touch,
To gain or lose it all.

And in the Empire of thine heart,
Where I should solely be,
If others do pretend a part
Or dare to vie with me,
Or Committees if thou erect
And go on such a score,
I'll laugh and sing at thy neglect,
And never love thee more.

But if thou wilt prove faithful then,
And constant of thy word,
I'll make thee glorious by my pen
And famous by my sword.
I'll serve thee in such noble ways
Was never heard before;
I'll crown and deck thee all with bays
And love thee more and more.

In that poem is contained more than an entreaty to his wife
not to admit approaches from Calvinist synods and committees; it is his whole philosophy, especially the second verse.
Only his generosity does not shine through. He forgave two

kings who let him down, and went, even to the scaffold, forgiving. And, though he could not always control his troops, he refused to let those prisoners who were under his control at Blair Castle be massacred in retaliation for the atrocities committed by his opponents after Philiphaugh. At his execution "his speech was full of composure and his carriage as sweet as ever I saw a man in all my days". His last words were;

> I have no more to say to you but that I desire your charity and your prayers; I shall pray for you all. I leave my soul to God, my service to my Prince, my goodwill to my friends, my love and charity to you all.

His body was dismembered and exhibited in the four principal cities of the realm but the remains were later collected and buried in St Giles though none now knows exactly where. And after the Restoration, there was a grand funeral. After a lying-in-state in the chapel of Holyrood, his body was carried by fourteen peers up the Canongate, attended by his Graham kinsmen, while the trained bands of Edinburgh "in gallant order ranged both sides of the streets".

The Scots under Alexander Leslie played a notable part in the defeat of the King at Marston Moor in 1644 but they were disappointed in their hope of seeing a truly Presbyterian system established in England and thus Charles thought it worth while to throw himself on their mercy. It was to no avail; in spite of a Scottish contingent commanded by Hamilton, he was beaten at Preston and his execution followed in January 1649.

After Charles's execution, there was a time when even Argyll was ready to fight for his son, mistakenly believing him to be a Covenanted King, but, in spite of the success of David Leslie (Alexander's nephew) in outmanoeuvring Cromwell at Dunbar, that battle was lost; and the next year, 1651, another Royalist defeat at Worcester sealed the issue. In spite of that there was one last desperate effort under Glencairn and Middleton in 1653–4 (joined by Montrose's son) but it was

60. *Earl of Glencairn, Kilmaurs, Kilmarnock. Moderate in religion, he was made Chancellor by Charles II. His monument is in the family aisle— Renaissance in style but simple; busts of himself and his wife, with smaller ones of his eight children, are framed within Corinthian pillars.*

crushed by Monk's army at Dalnaspidal in 1654.

Under the Protectorate, taxation was heavy and the foreigner was resented, but according to Burnet "many people reckoned those years of usurpation a time of great peace and prosperity". And, in the end, it was from Coldstream in Scotland[1] that Monk marched to proclaim the Restoration— though Scotland got no say in the terms! One of them proved to be the trial and execution of the Marquess of Argyll. He was the ablest (if not the most lovable) of a long line of able chiefs of the Clan Campbell. At first a servant of Charles I, he then led the Covenanters against him. A politician rather than a soldier, his position forced him into nominal command in the field for which he was unfitted, and at Inverlochy where Montrose arrived so unexpectedly, he escaped before the defeat of his men. Then, for a time, he treated with Charles II and per-

[1] Coldstream has a pleasant garden, overlooking the Tweed, commemorating the raising of the Coldstream Guards.

61. *Argyll's body was dismembered according to the barbarous laws of the times, but eventually the remains were buried in the family vault at Kilmun, Argyll. This sumptuous marble monument was erected in the nineteenth century in a bay in the north aisle of St Giles, Edinburgh. Above it, a stained-glass window displays the coats of arms of some of the Covenanter leaders.*

62. *The Mercat Cross, Aberdeen. Some mercat crosses, such as the seventeenth-century ones at Airth (Elphinstone) and Kincardine-on-Forth (Graham) were family monuments, but Aberdeen Cross has been chosen partly because it is exceptionally fine, partly because the panels on the parapet bear medallions with the heads of James I–VII, Mary, Queen of Scots, and Charles I and II. On top is a unicorn holding a shield with the royal arms. It dates from 1685.*

The railing round the cross is no longer there; this rather out-of-date photograph has been selected because it shows most clearly the heads of those monarchs nearest in time to the erection of the cross.

sonally crowned him at Scone, only to break with him again and accept Cromwell. Not surprisingly, he has been called a turncoat but in fact he was always consistent in fighting for the maintenance of the Presbyterian Church in Scotland; and his faith was genuinely held and regularly practised to the extent of spending one to two long hours every day in Bible reading and prayer. It was only when he discovered how false were Charles II's professions of Presbyterianism that he abandoned him. Like his great rival, he made a dignified end in 1661, after spending his waiting days writing a book of advice for his son. It was no Puritan tract and commended to him the

63. *The statue to Charles II, Parliament Square, Edinburgh. First erected in 1685 and said to be the oldest equestrian statue in lead in the country, Charles is depicted "in the Roman manner, like one of the Caesars, almost naked and so without spurs and without stirrups". The construction of the statue was not so lasting as the Romans would have made it. In George III's reign an attempt to preserve it was made by painting it white, provoking Boswell to comment:*

> *The milk-white steed is well enough,*
>   *But why thus daub the man all over,*
> *And to the swarthy Stewart give*
>   *The cream complexion of Hanover?*

In George IV's reign it was strengthened with timber inside, but it had to receive further remedial treatment in this century.

game of golf, of which he himself had been a lover, and riding.

Charles II probably cared as little about the religion of Scotland as he did about everything else to do with her, but his supporters ensured the restoration of an Episcopal establishment. Some Presbyterians acquiesced, others bided their time, but there was a minority of extreme Calvinists who preferred to take to the hills to worship God rather than have any truck with bishops. These Covenanters were especially strong in the south-west and in Fife. Lauderdale was at first in London as the King's principal adviser on Scottish affairs with Glencairn as Chancellor in Edinburgh and Middleton as Lord High Commissioner. Rothes succeeded the latter but he lost favour as a result of his too brutal treatment of Covenanter prisoners rounded up after the skirmish of Rullion Green. Then, for a time, Lauderdale permitted greater leniency but "The Killing Times" soon returned. Almost as great a tragedy was that no accommodation was reached between the Episcopalians and the more moderate Presbyterians in view of the fact that there was at this time very little difference between their forms of worship; only later did the Episcopalians return to more Arminian ways. One of the villains undoubtedly was that strange creature James Sharp. As Presbyterian Professor of

64. Archbishop Sharp's tomb in Holy Trinity Church, St Andrews. Sharp was murdered on Magus Muir on 3rd May 1679, and this is a tribute from his nephew who rather overstated his case in a Latin inscription to: "The holiest of bishops, sagest of state counsellors, most saintly of martyrs . . . whom the University acknowledged as professor of theology and philosophy, the church as priest, teacher and leader, Scotland as Prime Minister, Britain as the advocate of the Restoration of His Most Gracious Majesty Charles II." The tomb is of Dutch design and imposing rather than beautiful. Sharp, in white marble, kneels on a black sarcophagus, while an angel holds a crown above his head. Beneath, hidden in this illustration by the railings, there is a tablet in low relief showing him being killed in the presence of his daughter, but the figures are, with one exception, wooden.

A more fortunate bishop of the same period was Scougall of Aberdeen. The area in which he served was more sympathetic to Episcopacy; he aroused less hostility and died peacefully before 1689. His tomb is in St Machar's Cathedral.

Here lies Interred the Heads of LAUR HAY
and ANDREW PITULLOCH - who
Suffered martyrdom at EDINR July 13, 1681
for adhering to the word of GOD & Scotlands
covenanted work of Reformation, and also
one of the Hands of DAVID HACKSTON
of Rathillot, who was most cruelly murdered
at EDINR July 30th 1680
for the same cause.

Divinity at St Andrews and former minister of Crail, he had been sent to London to plead the cause of that church to Charles; he returned as Archbishop of St Andrews. For this change of coat and for his subsequent mercilessness, he paid a terrible penalty nineteen years later when he was dragged from his coach and murdered on Magus Muir; no less terrible was the revenge taken by the Government on his assassins.

When Charles died and his Roman Catholic brother James became King, the ninth Earl of Argyll tried to raise the country to preserve the Protestant Succession; but he had misjudged the strength of the Government and followed his father to the scaffold. And when James's policy in England collapsed and he fled that country, it was by no means certain that Scotland would accept William of Orange in his place. Claverhouse raised an army of Highlanders for James and won an early victory at Killiecrankie;[2] but he was killed in the hour of victory and his troops failed in an attack on Dunkeld and soon melted away. The Williamite regiment that defeated them was

[2] Site in the care of the National Trust for Scotland.

65. The Covenanters. There are many memorials to the Covenanters, especially in the south-west where they were strongest, but one from Fife is of some interest in that it commemorates Hackston, one of Sharp's murderers, and also illustrates the bitterness that Sharp's persecution left behind. On one side of the stone it declares that here lie interred the heads of Laurence Hay and Andrew Pitulloch who suffered martyrdom in 1681 and one of the hands of David Hackston, "cruelly murdered in Edinburgh on 30th July 1680" (i.e. executed for his part in Sharp's murder). On the reverse is:

> *Our persecutors filled with rage*
> *Their brutish fury to assuage*
> *Took heads and hands of martyrs off*
> *That they might be the people's scoff.*
> *They Hackston's body cut asunder*
> *And set it up a world's wonder*
> *In several places to proclaim*
> *These monsters gloried in their shame.*

Scott's Old Mortality was based on Robert Paterson, 1712–1800, who devoted his life to caring for the inscriptions to Galloway Covenanters. He is buried at Balmaclellan near Dumfries, where his wife kept a school.

66. *Statue of William III by the Cathedral, Glasgow, presented 1734 by the Hon. James M'Crae, Governor of Madras. For many years it stood near the Tolbooth where it may be seen in the lively picture of the Trongate 1826 by John Knox—a picture familiar to many as the dust cover of Rosalind Mitchison's fascinating book* Life in Scotland.

When traffic increased, the statue was taken down and stored, and it was only re-erected in 1926 at the insistence of the Grand Orange Lodge of Scotland.

Glasgow Cathedral has one of the few Scottish brasses—albeit a very small one of a knight kneeling—the Minto memorial on the south wall of the nave.

later to be known as the Cameronians.[3] In Parliament, too, the Protestant interest led by the third Duke of Hamilton prevailed.

To strike terror into the hearts of the Highlanders who were equally feared by William's Lowland advisers and by the King himself, the MacDonalds of Glencoe[4] were singled out to be made an example. William gave his specific consent but the manner in which the slaughter under trust was undertaken did not win him any love even amongst their enemies. Nor did a series of bad harvests; though they were hardly his fault, they became known as "William's bad years". He must, however, bear some of the blame for the continued exclusion of Scotland from trade with the colonies of England and for the deliberate strangling of Scotland's attempt to found her own outlet for trade in the New World with a colony at Darien. Only in the matter of religion did the majority of Scots benefit; this time they found a more persuasive envoy to London, and a more convinced one, in Carstares, and his task was made easier by the fact that Bishop Rose of Edinburgh antagonized William by declaring that he could only offer him allegiance "so far as law, conscience or reason will allow". Presbyterianism was once again the Established religion of Scotland.

Anne succeeded William in 1702. She was a Stewart but she lived in England and was advised principally by English ministers. Constitutional disputes arose over who should succeed her in view of the fact that there was no direct heir after the death of her son the Duke of Gloucester. The English Whigs and some of the Tories wanted a Hanoverian to ensure the Protestant Succession and exclude the firmly Roman Catholic James Edward. The Scots refused—unless some of their grievances were remedied.

The resulting compromise—the Treaty of Union of 1707—seemed to the English to be a generous gesture on their behalf; trade was to be opened freely to the Scots; they were to keep their own legal system and their own Established

[3] In 1892 a statue of their first Colonel, John, Earl of Angus, was erected at Douglas, Lanarkshire, near the place of the first mustering in 1689.
[4] Site in the care of the National Trust for Scotland.

67. Bothwell Church, Lanarkshire. The third Duke of Hamilton was a Councillor to Charles II and James VII, but was one of the first to transfer his allegiance to William. He presided over the presided over the Convention held in Edinburgh to declare the throne of Scotland vacant: "Rough and sullen but candid and sincere". This tomb was designed by James Smith who had worked on Charles II's remodelling of Holyrood Palace. The best parts are the heraldry above and the imagery of war below.

Church; the financial settlement and the representation they were offered at Westminster seemed fair. Unfortunately, to many Scots things looked very different. Edinburgh had already lost its King and Court, together with the pageantry and the business that went with them, in 1603, and ambitious men had already discovered that those who sought political influence (and the wealth that often went with it) must live in the South. Now the Scottish Parliament was to go too. And, if the Westminster Parliament were to be sovereign, there was precious little security that any safeguards in the Treaty would prove lasting—a fact that became apparent all too soon. The

68. *The monument to the second Duke of Queensberry, Durisdeer Church, Dumfries. John van Nost's tomb is not unlike that of the third Duke of Hamilton in style but is a great deal more pleasing— except perhaps for the somewhat un-comfortable posture of the Duke himself. He had been an early adherent of William's, leaving James at the same time as Prince George (Queen Anne's husband) and Ormonde. And he proved a skilful negotiator both as Commissioner of the Estates after the Darien disaster and when working for the Union.*

second Duke of Argyll and the second Duke of Queensberry (a Douglas) were amongst those who supported the Union, as was George MacKenzie, first Earl of Cromarty;[5] the fourth Duke of Hamilton temporized.

[5] MacKenzie had a forty-foot obelisk erected over his grave—it is said, in order to frustrate the declared intention of his wife to dance upon it. Another, rather later, eccentric had an equally good reason for an unusual memorial. A retired judge of the East India Company owned a wide estate at Kinettles in Angus—but only in view of his marriage and "so long as his wife remained above ground". Since the lady predeceased him, the judge placed her coffin in a glass case in a mausoleum—above ground—and so remained in possession!

Certainly the Union[6] deserves some of the credit for the gradual increase in prosperity during the eighteenth century. In agriculture, the Lowlands benefited most as a result of the introduction of new crops (especially potatoes and turnips) and of improved implements; by the consolidation and enclosure of holdings, and by better drainage. But, as elsewhere, this was often at the expense of the little man who tended to lose his independence and become a wage earner, uncertain of employment from season to season. Yields in the Highlands increased too, and there was a swift and remarkable rise in population.

Trade expanded; first sugar, then linen and tobacco, though the wars with France that continued throughout the 1700s caused periodical interruptions. As islands in the West Indies changed hands from time to time fortunes were lost as well as made, but in spite of individual bankruptcies Glasgow especially grew in size and wealth.

As well as memorials to the soldiers and statesmen who were to the fore in these years of domestic and foreign wars, there were civilian entrepreneurs such as Sir George Bruce who died in 1642 and William Duff.

[6] The Union is commemorated in a remarkably beautiful ceiling at Castle Menzies, Weem, Perthshire—home of the family of Illustration 53.

69. The memorial to Sir George Bruce of Carnock in Culross Abbey, Fife. Bruce developed the coal seams round Culross and earned the gratitude of posterity by building the splendid Culross Palace—as has the National Trust for Scotland by restoring it. The monument has been criticized on the grounds that its architectural orders are more picturesque than correct, and by Ian Finlay as pompous, though he allows some merit to the smaller but individual figures of Bruce's three sons and five daughters. For myself I prefer, and find considerable dignity in, the life-size effigies of their parents. They have been attributed to the Englishman Edward Marshall, later Master Mason to Charles II, but the tomb itself is signed by a John Gibson who may have been a local man. If so, it might account for this memorial being somewhat simpler in design than the contemporary ones of Kinnoull, Scone and Dunbar. Or tomb and figures may be from different hands.

Another Bruce, Sir William, was the leading architect of the seventeenth century and a very influential one. He was employed by Charles II on the rebuilding of Holyrood. In the great houses he designed for himself at Balcaskie in Fife, and at Kinross, he designed house and garden to complement each other. Both are still inhabited, and Kinross may be regarded as a monument both to Bruce and to Sir Basil Montgomery who in 1902 reclaimed house and garden magnificently from the derelict condition into which they had fallen.

These years also saw the coming of a new type of memorial, the elaborate family aisle added to a parish church. One at Kilbirnie, Ayrshire, built by John, Viscount Garnock, is a gallery in oak, very grand, very heraldic, comfortably private and completely dominating, of around 1703. The estate was a Crawford property entailed on Margaret Crawford who married a Lindsay; eight panels show the distinguished nature of her lineage, eight that of his.[7] At Pitsligo in Aberdeenshire the Forbes aisle is smaller but equally ornate. Illustration 70 shows the Montgomery aisle from Skelmorlie, Ayrshire.

[7] At Kilbirnie there is also an almost entirely enclosed monument of intermediate design to Thomas Crawford and his wife dated 1594.

70. The Montgomery Aisle, Skelmorlie, 1636. Built by Sir Robert Montgomery, who died in 1651 penitent for various acts of revenge which he had committed, it takes the form of a gallery over a tomb-house. It may have been designed abroad but executed by local craftsmen. The wooden painted roof has lively pictures of the four seasons, Adam and Eve, Jacob and Esau, the signs of the Zodiac and, remarkably, coats of arms for the twelve tribes of Israel. Sir Robert's successor, Sir James Montgomery of Skelmorlie, was chosen as representative of the barons or gentry for the delegation sent to London to offer the crown of Scotland to William, but later he plotted against him and was detected and ended his life as a fugitive.

143

71. *Little is changed in Parliament Hall, Edinburgh, since this view was
drawn of nineteenth-century lawyers promenading beneath their august
predecessors. Forbes's distinguished statue by Roubiliac shows him with
outstretched arm. His tomb is in Greyfriars Churchyard. For other statues
in Parliament House see page 200.*

SEVEN

The Eighteenth Century

In the eighteenth century, the emphasis moves away from the politicians for reasons already discussed. Indeed, between the Act of Union 1707 and the beginnings of agitation for reform in the 1790s, Scottish elections and the members they threw up were "managed" on behalf of the second and third Dukes of Argyll and their successors Bute and North, Pitt and Dundas. For the two Dukes, their manager north of the Border was Duncan Forbes of Culloden whose career spanned the '15 and the '45; active in opposition to both, he was, more than any other one man, responsible for the failure of Prince Charles Edward. He persuaded a number of undecided Chiefs not to join the rising, and others actually to throw in their lot with the Government. He worked tirelessly to see that the Government forces should be adequately supplied, paid, and used to the best effect. And he raised companies at his own expense. In return, he received neither recompense nor thanks, partly because he had protested against the brutalities of Cumberland (for whom in England, Handel was composing "See the Conquering Hero comes").

In the popular mind, the eighteenth century is above all else that of Jacobitism, but, critical as the risings were to those immediately concerned, their failure had less effect on the majority of Scotsmen than the new found peace in the High-lands and the increasing prosperity in the Lowlands. And, since the risings brought ruin to those who led them, such memorials as exist, tend to be later in date, as, for instance, those marking Mar's headquarters in 1715 at Sheriffmuir and the raising of the Stewart standard in 1745 at Glenfinnan. But both are worth visiting if only for the lovely views over the surrounding countryside. Flora MacDonald is com-memorated by a cross at Kilmuir, Isle of Skye, where she was buried and by a statue before the Castle in Inverness.

So far as the Highlands were concerned, the death of Claverhouse, the stunning effect of Glencoe, and the heavy Hanoverian hand which spread outward from its base in Argyll, brought comparative peace and a suppression of cattle stealing. Under Wade and Caulfield, a network of military roads was constructed, and independent companies were formed of well-disposed Highlanders who alone were allowed to wear the kilt and to carry arms. These were later embodied into the Black Watch and were the forerunners of other High-land regiments which won distinction in the American Wars. The bridge which Wade built at Aberfeldy in 1733 stands appropriately beside the nineteenth-century statue com-memorating the embodiment of the Black Watch in 1739.

Agriculture throughout the land benefited from domestic peace. In the Highlands, black cattle were increasingly exported to be fattened in England, and the introduction of the black-faced sheep, and then the Cheviot, at first proved an advantage; though the old native breed produced very fine wool, there was little of it, and less meat, on the beasts. Only later did the increasing demand for wool and mutton lead to the Clearances for sheep runs. The Lowlands saw an even greater growth of prosperity as new methods were being introduced. The old joint tenancy farm in runrig was giving way to a larger unit, its fields enclosed and better drained; there were more efficient ploughs, new crops and greater yields. The potato improved diet all over the country and the turnip provided food for both man and beast. Scottish forestry and Scottish gardening became famous.

Meanwhile, as methods of banking developed and capital became more readily available, trade with the New World

72. *The Glenfinnan Memorial, Loch Shiel. This tower, now in the care of the National Trust for Scotland, was erected by Macdonald of Glenaladale in 1815 on the spot where Charles Edward raised his standard after landing with seven companions—the "Eight Men of Moidart". Queen Victoria described it as "very ugly, looking like a lighthouse with a statue on top", but even she was impressed by the loveliness of the loch side. The situation is superb, and a conservation agreement with the Trust has secured the future of twenty-eight acres around the monument. A Visitors' Centre provides an exposition of the Prince's march from Glenfinnan, south to Derby, and back to Culloden. The site of Culloden in Inverness-shire is also cared for by the NTS, who have been at great pains to enable the visitor, by maps and a relief model, to follow the lie of the land and how the battle was fought, and to find the graves of the slain, the cairns and the other monuments. Not the least remarkable of the relics of the battle is the blue banner of the Appin Stewarts which today hangs alongside the colours of its old opponents, Barrel's Regiment, in the Scottish United Services Museum at Edinburgh Castle. After seventeen Stewarts from Appin and Morvern had died defending it, one of their comrades, Donald Livingstone, escaped from the field with it wound round his body.*

147

gave Glasgow and the west an opportunity to exploit the natural advantages of the Clyde, and to improve them. Sugar, tobacco and cotton were imported, textiles exported. The growth of the linen industry led to the further development of other manufacturing towns in the Central Belt such as Dunfermline and Paisley. Edinburgh continued to flourish and fortunes were made even in the north. Such a one was that of William Duff of Dipple, 1653–1722, who started his trading career with £500, married advantageously and ended with extensive lands, a rental of £6,500 per year and £30,000 in cash, having established for himself a close hold on trade between northern Scotland and the Netherlands. His house still exists in Elgin; that of his son, who became Earl of Fife in 1759, was the mansion of Duff House, Banff, designed by William Adam (Illustration 75).

There was growth too, as the century progressed, in the coal and iron industries which, with Watt's steam engine, were going to dominate the Scotland of Queen Victoria. Though ideas and capital were often produced by great landowners, this was the age of the middling sort of man, the professional—and, be it added, the scholar and the artist.

James Watt did more than any other one man to influence the course of the Industrial Revolution. Born in Greenock in 1736, he became an instrument maker but would probably have been prevented from following that craft by the Hammermen's Guild, had not the University taken him into their employ. When he was repairing a model of Newcomen's steam engine, he hit on the idea of a separate condenser to make it more efficient, and then on other improvements. In due course his pumping engine was patented and, in conjunction with Matthew Boulton, it was developed and produced in Birmingham; it soon superseded Newcomen's. Apart from this far-reaching discovery, Watt was an extremely versatile man who early in life had been engaged on survey work for the Forth-Clyde canal, and on improving the harbours at Greenock and Port Glasgow; later he devised and patented numerous useful inventions, among them a

73. *James Watt in George Square, Glasgow. Watt's is the statue nearest the camera in this picture—cast in bronze in 1832 by Sir Francis Chantrey, who also did one of him for Greenock. Watt is commemorated by a statue in Edinburgh University and by the naming of the Heriot Watt University. Not all the statues in George Square are very distinguished, least of all Marochetti's Queen Victoria prancing on horseback in her crown. But Prince Albert is better, seen on the left of the photograph, and Scott on his column designed by John Greenshields and executed by Handyside and Ritchie. On the whole the soldiers (centre right) come off best—Sir John Moore by Flaxman, 1819 (Illustration 81), and Colin Campbell, Lord Clyde, by Foley, 1868. Gladstone is by W. H. Thorneycroft, 1902, and Sir Robert Peel (once Lord Rector of the University), by John Mossman, 1859, Burns by George Ewing, 1877. On the far side of the Square stands the 1914–18 Cenotaph.*

149

smokeless engine and a governor, not to mention a device for copying sculpture. George Stephenson who developed the steam locomotive was also of Scottish origin, his grandfather having been a Roxburghshire shepherd, but he was born in Newcastle.

The eighteenth century saw new life stirring in the Scottish universities. Their mathematicians, Simson, MacLaurin[1] and Stewart, outstripped those of Oxford and Cambridge, wealthier though those foundations were. Robertson the historian and the philosopher Hume[2] were European figures. Adam Smith inaugurated the "dismal science" of Economics but, in fact, his own *Wealth of Nations* is far from dismal; nor were his lectures, though he is said to have been dullish company on occasions. Something may have been due to his extreme vagueness; at any rate his friends forgave him for he was immensely beloved and his epigrams were worth waiting for—"It is worth sometimes going to church for the pleasure of coming out". He was buried in the Canongate Churchyard but his best memorial is the Adam Smith Centre in his birthplace Kirkcaldy, Fife.

Surgery (if not always medicine) was becoming a science. James IV, the amateur dentist and bleeder, had granted a Charter to the Royal College of Surgeons which had its first Hall in 1697. Its lintel and pediment are preserved in their present Hall.

There were three generations of Monro to teach in Edinburgh; the son founded the School of Anatomy there. Of the grandson, it is told that he preferred to use his grandfather's lecture notes but could never remember to omit the somewhat improbable phrase "When I was a student at Leiden in 1718. . . ." Among the pupils of Monro (grandfather) was William Cullen, who laid the foundation for the study of the nervous system, and among *his* pupils was William Hunter, most famous of all the eighteenth-century surgeons especially

[1] Buried in Greyfriars' Churchyard.
[2] Old Calton Burial Ground has his circular tomb in Edinburgh.

74. *Surgeons' Hall, Nicolson Street, Edinburgh, 1832. It was designed by W. H. Playfair, who also chose the Greek style for the National Gallery and for the ill-fated National Memorial (after the Napoleonic Wars) on Calton Hill but worked in other traditions for New College and Donald-son's Hospital.*

for his work in obstetrics. Though he (and his brother John) spent much of their lives in England, he left his collection of specimens to form the basis of a museum of international repute to Glasgow, his old university. The Edinburgh Surgeons' Hall also has a remarkable museum for those who have the stomach to look at monstrous births and suchlike, and relics of the great nineteenth-century surgeons, and a plaque telling how, when the Polish universities were destroyed in the Second World War, and Polish professors were killed in concentration camps, Edinburgh University gave young Polish students the chance to train in medicine, and subsequently to give of their talents to healing in Scotland.

In those days, it was outside the academic world that architects received their training. William Adam (1689–1748) of Kirkcaldy learnt his trade as Clerk of Works to Sir William Bruce, and went on to build great houses. He was the last

75. *The wings to Duff House were never completed, but the central block (now being restored) is "the most arresting of all William Adam's surviving works; a medieval castle in Baroque dress" (see J. G. Dunbar,* The Historic Architecture of Scotland*). It is a fitting memorial to him. For Adam's patron see page 148.*

major Scottish architect, says J. G. Dunbar, whose work was fundamentally different from that of contemporary designers on the other side of the Border. Drum House, Edinburgh, and Duff House, Banff, are his, and—above all—Hopetoun House, West Lothian (though it was completed after his death by his son Robert).

William was buried in Greyfriars' Churchyard, Edinburgh; Robert, like so many distinguished Scots since the Union, in Westminster Abbey. But, though he worked much in England, he was also prolific in Scotland, notably in the New Town of Edinburgh, in Charlotte Square and the Register House. He was much influenced by his stay in Italy, 1754–62, but he also experimented with castellated motifs as at Mellerstain.

76. *The Register House, Edinburgh, begun by Robert Adam in 1774 but completed by other hands, as was his design for the University. The statue of Wellington in the foreground dates from 1852 and is by Sir John Steell, a native of Aberdeen, who was also responsible for the statues of Dr Chalmers in George Street, Prince Albert in Charlotte Square and Scott in the Princes Street monument.*

Of the poets of this Golden Age, Allan Ramsay and Robert Fergusson were writing in Scots, and Duncan Ban MacIntyre and Alexander MacDonald in Gaelic. Ramsay's monument was erected in Princes Street Gardens, eighteen tons of Carrara marble (by Sir John Steell), 1858; Fergusson's humbler stone in Canongate Churchyard was placed there by Burns fifteen years after his death in 1774. MacIntyre, born in Glenorchy in 1724, found most of his inspiration in his native hills while a gamekeeper, but ended his days as a member of the Edinburgh Town Guard. His stone circular monument has no special merit in itself but it has a wonderful setting near Dalmally, Argyll. Meanwhile Ramsay's son, also Allan, 1713–84, was a painter, paving the way for Raeburn, as Smollett in his novels did for Scott, but both settled in London. Smollett trained as a physician and served as a naval surgeon at Cartagena, but he lost faith in the medicines of his day which were as useless as they were unpalatable. As he said to one lady: "If you have time to play at being ill, I have no leisure to play at curing you." He had turned to writing as more lucrative. Even so, he was very poor when he died, abroad. *Humphrey Clinker* was occasioned by a visit to his homeland. His memorial is a Tuscan column at Renton, Dumbarton, his birthplace, with an impressive Latin inscription by Dr Johnson.

So much for the figures of national renown, but notable memorials are no longer confined to such. Once again a new century brings a new fashion in monuments—headstones standing over the graves of the middling sort of folk, ministers, merchants, craftsmen. It is true that a few small headstones carved with crosses survive from the Middle Ages as at North Berwick and a few recumbent slabs, comparable to those of the West Highland tradition, (though seldom so beautiful), as on a stone at Roxburgh and on another at Smeaton, where alongside a foliate cross are a sword and a pair of shears. And there is a rather larger number of such stones from the seventeenth century—though, for the most part, monuments of that date tend to resemble those which had been erected *inside* churches until the Reformation discouraged the practice—table and chest tombs, wall tablets and recumbent slabs. St Andrews Cathedral Burial Ground and Museum are particularly rich in all types of early monuments and, on a lesser scale, so too is Abercorn.[3] Then suddenly the demand for the older types dies away, and headstones carved in low relief proliferate, the work of local masons who followed no set pattern books and so gave to "each humble stone an individuality, a meaningfulness".

Betty Willsher and Doreen Hunter have recently published a fascinatingly informative and splendidly illustrated survey, *18th Century Gravestones*, Canongate Publishing Ltd, 1978.

---

[3] Crichton also has some good memorials of seventeenth-century craftsmen, and Cranston a very early slab with a cross with two traverses.

77. A very
fine Abraham
and Isaac stone
commemorating
Donald Richie,
sometime
tailor, from
Lundie,
Angus, 1759.

Two of the largest and earliest which they include are the "Faith, Hope and Charity" stone of 1651 from the Greyfriars' Churchyard, Perth, a tailor's monument packed with emblems and small figures, and the Faichney Memorial from Innerpeffray, Perthshire, 1707. Here the mason himself is portrayed with his wife, while the lower panel containing his coat of arms is flanked by small figures of his ten children, the boys in the kilt and the girls in long dresses.

There are certain favourite Biblical scenes, amongst them Adam and Eve (the authors have counted over thirty) and the sacrifice of Isaac of which they show a highly dramatic

78. The gravestone of John Murray, game-keeper, Kells, Kirkcud-bright, 1777.

79. Less frequently was the figure of the deceased portrayed. At Temple, Midlothian, there is a farmer, smartly dressed, with two of his children.

example from Lundie, Angus. Many stones carry emblems of mortality such as skulls, crossed bones, a skeleton, an hourglass and even Death himself (see the Arbroath Abbey Museum for an amusing example); and some have those of immortality, the winged soul, the angel of resurrection, and the Crown of Life. Most characteristic of all are the various emblems which show the occupation of the deceased. An illustration from Inverarity, Angus, has the hammer, tweezers, pliers, wrench and vice of a Hammerman, whose Guild included smiths, watchmakers, plumbers and gunmakers and, also, surprisingly, glovers and saddlers. The Weavers have a good loom at Kirkton of Monikie, Angus, and the Waulkmillers a stone of 1737 at Kirkmichael, Ayrshire, which has not only a fine pair of shears and a fulling pot, but also an apprentice working the machinery of the mill and the miller driving a plough to show that he had his own land. Bakers, shoemakers, mariners are represented, the ships naturally providing great scope for the mason. Perth has a splendid example and so too has Montrose. Of the many other occupations, we must limit ourselves to one. At Kells, Kirkcudbrightshire, a stone and its epitaph to a gamekeeper are both notable; the gun of 1777 is faithfully carved, as are the fishing rod, the powder flask, the retriever and the quarry (a pigeon?).

> Ah John what changes since I saw thee last
> Thy fishing and thy shooting days are past.
> Bagpipes and Hautboys thou canst sound no more.
> Thy nods, grimaces, winks, and pranks are o'er.
> Thy harmless, queerish, incoherent talk,
> Thy wild vivacity and trudging walk
> Will soon be quite forgot; thy joys on earth
> A snuff, a glass, riddles and noisy mirth
> Are vanished all. Yet blest I hope thou art
> For in thy station, weel thou played thy part.

He had lived well who could earn such a tribute.

80. *The National Memorial, Calton Hill, Edinburgh. This was intended
to be a great church, modelled on the Parthenon, but unfortunately only
enough money was raised to build the portico. Its architect was W. H.
Playfair, who likewise turned to Greece for the square monument in the
picture (to his uncle Professor Playfair) and for the circular memorial to
Burns, not in the picture but close by at the foot of the hill. The other*

EIGHT

The Years 1780–1830

The last two decades of the eighteenth century, and the first three of the nineteenth, were of such importance in themselves, and in the events that they led up to, that they deserve a section to themselves. The Agrarian and the Industrial Revolutions were gathering strength, the Intellectual Revolution had reached its peak and on them broke first the French Revolution and then the world-wide wars to which it gave rise. Macaulay, a London Scot, wrote of Frederick the Great that: "In order that he might rob a woman whom he had promised to defend, black men fought each other on the coasts of Coromandel and red men scalped each other by the Great Lakes of North America." The sentiment is no less true of Napoleon and as a result Scottish regiments, often commanded by Scottish generals, went out to earn fame in every continent. For the generals, Sir John Moore must stand representative and, for the rank and file, the National Memorial on Calton Hill, Edinburgh.

prominent memorial—the part-octagonal, part-circular tower—was erected to Lord Nelson in 1815. Glasgow is proud of the fact that it 'did' him rather earlier and rather more successfully.

There is no better view of the city of Edinburgh than that from Calton Hill on a summer's evening.

81. The statue to Sir John Moore, George Square, Glasgow. Moore was the greatest trainer of men that the British army has known and, if he had lived, might well have proved a more imaginative commander than Wellington. He was the first officer in high command to regard private soldiers as thinking human beings who could act on their own initiative and be relied on to fight in extended order, rather than as the scum of the earth whose feelings were best brutalized so that they should march unquestioning, shoulder to shoulder. He formed and trained a Light Division of Light Infantrymen and Riflemen who specialized in marksmanship and in swift marching, during the time when he was commanding the south coast of England against a possible invasion.

Military service took him much abroad but he remained a Scot at heart and always tried to get Scots for his own regiment, the 52nd Light Infantry. Lord Lynedoch, in admiration, formed his 90th Perthshire Volunteers as Light Infantry. Thus, when these were linked to the Cameronians, Scotland got (for a time) its only Rifle Regiment.

Wellington (by Steell) rides before the Register House in Edinburgh and (by Marochetti) in Royal Exchange Square, Glasgow. His victory at Waterloo named several Scottish villages and has a landmark monument near Crailing. But its most remarkable memorial was the planting of extensive woodlands at South Hall, Colintraive, Argyll, in the formations adopted by the troops on either side. Sadly, the timber did not survive the Second World War.

Of the Scottish commanders of the day, Sir Hector Munro, the victor of Negapatam, is worthy of special mention because the vast replica of the gate of that city which he constructed on the summit of Fyrish Hill, Alness, Easter Ross, 1782, was undertaken to provide work for those hit by recession. Others who made their mark were Crawford, who succeeded Moore in command of the Light Division, Baird of Seringapatam and Egypt[1] and Abercromby, who was killed at Aboukir, but not before he had secured the surrender of 20,000 Frenchmen;[2] Lord Lynedoch;[3] Elliott who defended Gibraltar and the fourth Earl of Hopetoun who has a statue in St Andrew Square, Edinburgh, and is also commemorated on the summit of Mount Hill, north-west of Cupar, Fife. At sea, Duncan saved his country at Camperdown[4] and Cochrane was brilliant if sometimes erratic.

Other Scotsmen won equal renown in less military fields. Lachlan Macquarrie[5] revolutionized the course of Australian history by insisting that those deportees who had served out their time should be accepted as full citizens, and MacArthur introduced the merino sheep. Minto was the forerunner of a long line of proconsuls in India. The town of Selkirk produced

---

[1] His widow built a model village at St Davids, Madderty, and a monument on Tomchastle Hill, Crieff, Perthshire.
[2] Abercromby is buried in St Paul's, London.
[3] Buried at Methven, Perthshire.
[4] Camperdown House and Park are his worthy memorial in Dundee. He was buried nearby at Lundie.
[5] His burial place in his native Mull belongs to the National Trust of Australia, but is looked after by the National Trust for Scotland.

(and commemorates) Mungo Park, explorer of the Niger, while the Earl of that name sought to find homes and a better life in Canada for some of those suffering from the Clearances. Different from all of the above was another traveller, David Douglas, 1798–1834. The son of a Scone stonemason, he showed such promise during his gardening apprenticeship that he was able to travel widely in the New World. There he discovered many unknown animals, birds and plants and amongst other seeds which he brought back to this country were those of the Douglas fir (and other conifers), many shrubs, *Lupin polyphyllus*, eschscholtzia, clarkia and nemophila. In 1962 a memorial garden was made for him on the North Inch, Perth, to take the place of his decaying stone in the churchyard of Old Scone.

At home, in spite of the dangers threatening the country, the arts reached their peak. Raeburn[6] was painting his portraits; Boswell published his life of Doctor Johnson, Scott his Waverley novels—and Burns lived and wrote and died.

Meanwhile the technological advance was immense. Watt's inventions were being refined and widely applied; a railway, as yet horse-drawn, ran from Kilmarnock to Troon; canals linked the Forth to the Clyde; roads were being built everywhere and being given an all-weather surface; Macadam, Rennie and Telford were at the height of their careers as civil engineers;[7] the first steamship, the *Comet*, sailed down the Clyde.[8] Fortunes were being made, especially in Glasgow. The wars had often meant disaster, but if "the red-coated Tobacco lords disappeared from the streets, their places were taken by grim stern-faced factory owners, wearing instead

[6] Raeburn is buried, inconspicuously, in the graveyard of St John's Episcopal Church Princes Street, Edinburgh, and there is a commemorative tablet on his studio in York Place.
[7] Commemorated at their birthplaces, Macadam at Moffat, Rennie at East Linton and Telford at Westerkirk respectively.
[8] Henry Bell who designed it and J. Robertson who built the engines have their obelisks at Helensburgh and at Neilston, Renfrewshire.

82. *The Burns Monument at Alloway, Ayr. Burns may have been a poor ploughman, but his father had managed to see that he got a good grounding in literature. He was well read not only in the older Scottish poets but in the fashionable English writers of the day; and he could read French and knew something of the Latin authors in translation. He was convivial, humorous and satirical, as well as superbly lyrical.*

He is, naturally, commemorated not only in Edinburgh but all over Scotland, especially in his native Ayrshire and the south-west—in the houses in which he was born, in Alloway, and died, in Dumfries, and at Irvine, Kilmarnock and Mauchline.

hard hats and drab grey". Cotton, hitherto the preserve of eastern Scotland, was the first to take off, but not far behind came the building of ships and locomotives, and then all the other forms of heavy industry that one thinks of as typical of nineteenth-century Scotland. The population nearly doubled, and an ever-increasing proportion of it came to live in the Central Belt, near the coal and, increasingly, it was swelled by Irish Roman Catholic immigrants.

In an age when the achievements were now those of professionals rather than of amateurs, of doers rather than possessors, it is not surprising to find a stirring of political consciousness, and a number of different strains demanding a radical shift in the balance of power. Yet not only the new poor, but the new rich, found themselves wholly excluded from political influence. It is significant, as Professor Ferguson has pointed out, that while in 1782 there were only eight newspapers in the whole of Scotland (and they chiefly of local concern) there were twenty-seven by 1790 and most had become intensely political. And their numbers were to increase.

Yet the franchise was even more restricted than in England. According to Logue, thirty county members were elected by a mere 2,662 voters while the remaining fifteen Scottish M.P.s were chosen by self-perpetuating and corrupt town councils of the Royal Burghs. Not surprisingly, the lawyer Henry Dundas, who had the "management" of affairs from 1784–1802, was able to deliver (in 1790) thirty-four of these forty-five seats to his master William Pitt; he was all-powerful. He did good work as Treasurer, and later First Lord, of the Admiralty but, during his first period of office, he had consented to a proposal that he should acquire some shares in the East India Company. When it came to light later that the money to buy the shares had been borrowed from Navy funds, Dundas had to face impeachment—the last statesman to do so. He was acquitted of knowing anything about the misappropriation but he retired into private life, to his estates near Comrie in Perthshire.

Being fearful of the consequences of any change (in the aftermath of the French Revolution) Melville and the Judges were able to stamp harshly on the Radicals of the day but not even the most vicious sentences of transportation were able to prevent agitation and rioting, especially in the 1790s[9] when

---

[9] Thomas Muir is commemorated in Old Calton Burial Ground; his Judge, Lord Braxfield, in R. L. Stevenson's *Weir of Hermiston*. Since Lord Cockburn's days, the latter has always been painted in the blackest colours. However, his reputation has recently been defended by C. M. H. Millar in the *Juridical Review* Vol. 24 (N.S.). The prosecutor in the case was a nephew of Henry's, Robert Dundas, who also has his statue in Parliament Hall.

83. The statue of Henry Dundas, first Viscount Melville, St Andrew Square, Edinburgh. Dundas has a splendidly sited memorial on a hill in Glen Lednock, near Comrie, and a statue by Chantrey in Parliament House, Edinburgh, but the monument most frequently seen is on this great column which dominates the other statues in George Street. These start with Prince Albert in Charlotte Square, then Thomas Chalmers (Illustration 90), William Pitt the Younger and George IV, seen in the foreground of this picture "going for a brisk walk with his sceptre". A statue to Henry's son and successor as manager of Scottish affairs, the second Viscount Melville, stands in Melville Street, Edinburgh.

the Government tried to make service in the militia compulsory, and after 1810 when there was widespread hunger as a result of low wages and high prices and lack of work owing to the interruption of cotton supplies from America. And there was, of course, nothing in the way of state help to cushion the hardship. Nor, so long as the Tories were in power, was there any likelihood of a reform of the franchise.

Yet social changes were in progress which sooner or later would have to be reckoned with. Unfortunately, even when

84. *The Scott Monument, Princes Street, Edinburgh. Scott, like Burns, owed much to the past; yet, like Burns, he also led a very full life in the present, in his social life and in his legal profession. Till middle age he was primarily a collector, re-writer and author of ballads and stirring narrative in verse, written often in the saddle and redolent of action. Then he gracefully yielded up his place as a poet to Byron (in spite of his birth, it seems difficult to think of Byron as a Scotsman*) and became a great novelist. He was, above all, a wonderful creator of character, particularly for his minor figures; his heroes and heroines are not always so arresting, and he does not reach the heights of tragedy. He too has monuments all over Scotland, the earliest in Perth. His tomb is in Dryburgh Abbey, as is Earl*

the Whigs did at last achieve power and passed the 1832 Reform Act, the social evils remained largely ignored. It was an age of *laissez-faire* when educated men took the optimistic view that all was proceeding, if only slowly, towards a millennium. In fact, though the rise in productivity had brought a rise in living standards to many—probably to the majority—of the working class, it had reduced some to abject penury in urban slums, and nearly all to an increased dependence on fluctuations in trading conditions. Some of such people, such as the handloom weavers, had previously enjoyed much greater independence in their daily lives and a much better chance of education. They, with their intellectual awareness, provided much of the backbone of both the political and the ecclesiastical radicalism of the day.

Haig's. His home at Abbotsford is open to the public. There is a column in George Square, Glasgow, but the best known is this mid-Victorian monument in Edinburgh's Princes Street, designed by G. M. Kemp. The foundations of the Gothic canopy rest on solid rock, fifty feet below street level. The portrait statue is by Sir John Steell, while a variety of hands have contributed to the sixty or so smaller figures representing characters from his books.

*Byron is commemorated in Aberdeen where, at the Grammar School, he received his early education before going on to Harrow.

85. *McCaig's Tower, Oban, Argyll. John Stuart McCaig was a banker who sought not only to perpetuate his own name by building an imitation of the Colosseum to overlook his native town but also to help skilled masons who at the end of the century lacked work. A nineteenth-century merchant who did not need to build his own memorial was Thomas Hay Marshall of*

NINE

The Nineteenth Century

Once again a new century sees a change in fashions. In the graveyard, we bid farewell to those small headstones of character, each one so lovingly carved by a local mason in his own manner, and enter the age of mass-production. The age of manuscripts (as it were) is succeeded by the age of printing. In the big cities, the new rich tried to outdo each other, in death, in a way that their natural caution forbade during their lifetime, and their sepulchral extravagance is seen at its most typical in the Glasgow Necropolis. By 1800 the older church-yards of that city had become so overcrowded that they were a scandal, and the Merchant House decided to devote some ground that they owned, just to the east of the Cathedral, to be developed as a resting place for "the high classes, and convert a property at present unfrequented and unproductive into a general resort and a lucrative source of profit to a Charitable Institution". The hill of Fir Park had already been crowned with a vast statue to John Knox in 1825 and this was soon followed by the earliest interments in the 1830s. Each design had to be submitted for the aesthetic approval of the Merchants. At first they favoured the Greek style, but the

Perth, during whose Provostship the size of the North Inch was doubled, two fine new terraces were built and the old Perth Academy opened. His grateful fellow citizens subscribed handsomely to erect a statue in George Street and a new building which houses a museum.

86. *The Wallace Monument, Logie, Stirling. There are notable statues of Wallace at Aberdeen, Dryburgh, Lanark, Ayr and elsewhere, but the national one is this vast pseudo-medieval tower, designed by J. T. Rochead in the mid-nineteenth century. It stands on the top of Abbey Craig overlooking the old bridge of Stirling. It was on this crag that Wallace encamped the night before the Battle of Stirling Brig. (Incidentally, the bridge in the foreground of the picture, though the oldest and one of the finest in Scotland, dates only from the fifteenth century; that of Wallace's day was of wooden construction.)*

The tower itself is 220 feet high, and at its base its walls are 18 feet thick; from its summit, Ben Lomond can be seen to the west, and the Fife Lomonds to the east, right across the waist of Scotland. Inside the tower are three halls, one above the other. They contain collections of historical interest including a great two-handed sword (traditionally Wallace's but really of a later date) and a series of busts of distinguished Scots, most of them by D. W. Stevenson.

Not far away, beneath the Castle Rock of Stirling, are somewhat pedestrian statues of three of the leading personalities of the Scottish Reformation, John Knox, Andrew Melville and Alexander Henderson; only Henderson has any strength. (Henderson was minister of Leuchars, the lovely Romanesque church which has memorials to the Bruces of Earlshall, and Moderator of the General Assembly which abolished Episcopacy.) But there is plenty of character in the little statue of John Cowane which stands over the doorway of his seventeenth-century Hospital.

Egyptian and the Gothic were also essayed and, in at least one case, the Moorish. For most people, the Necropolis will be valued chiefly for its wonderful view on a sunny day, past the Cathedral to the city beyond, but its temples and obelisks, its broken pillars and angels and urns, its "elegance, opulence, pathos and vulgarity . . . give a wonderful insight into the trends, sympathies and sensibilities of the Victorians".[1] New burial grounds such as this and the Old Calton in Edinburgh were not appendages to churches but were to be available to all, irrespective of their religious attachments. A rather later graveyard at Arbroath is noted for its elaborately sculptured chapel, the style of which was christened by George Scott Moncrieff "Late Presbyterian".

Apart from the Victorian style of graveyard, there is another development in the proliferation of statues as tributes to memorability. Hitherto we have seen effigies on tombs but only isolated statues of monarchs—two (originally four) at Glamis and those of Charles II and William of Orange; there is nothing even nearly contemporary of the sort to Wallace or Bruce, Knox or Montrose. Now, not only these folk heroes get their statues but every notable figure, even non-Scots such as Nelson, Wellington and the younger Pitt, and a good many not very notable personages too, not to mention Greyfriars Bobby and Queen Victoria's pet dogs. Pitt was the first, and one of the most deserving; his statue by Chantrey was erected in George Street, Edinburgh, in 1803. Then Nelson on Glasgow Green in 1806 (an obelisk, not a statue) and in the same year at Forres (a tower on Cherryhill) and then the spate. In Glasgow, Sir John Moore 1819, Knox 1825 and Watt 1832; in Edinburgh, Dundas 1821, Burns on Calton Hill 1830 and then, like Scott, all over Scotland, Perth getting in first. Glasgow

---

[1] A fascinating survey of the Necropolis—of its development and of the styles and materials favoured—may be consulted in the Glasgow Room of the Mitchell Library, Glasgow, an unpublished thesis by Alexander Walsh, "The Glasgow Necropolis", 1979. John Baird, John Bryce, and David and Thomas Hamilton are all represented by work in the Necropolis.

put Scott on the top of a column in George Square which had been meant for George III.

The years 1780–1830 had been the Golden Age of Scottish poetry and painting, biography and the novel. The portrait painters had their afterglow in Wilkie,[2] supreme in his own line of character and country life, and in some competent landscape painters; and the sculptors of the period found plenty of commissions for their naturalistic studies. And Boswell was followed by John Gibson Lockhart whose *Life of Scott* may itself almost be regarded as a monument were it not for the fact that "monumental" as an epithet for a book seems to be regarded as an insult. But Burns found no really distinguished successors; nor did Scott, though Crockett[3] and the other sentimental writers of the Kailyard School were widely read in their day. Robert Louis Stevenson[4] still is, but though he died in 1894, he seems more typical of Edwardian than of Victorian writing. The two writers who have best survived are the historians Macaulay and Carlyle. Both were Anglo-Scots but Carlyle's birthplace at Ecclefechan is cared for by the National Trust for Scotland.

Towards the end of the century, Charles Rennie Macintosh as an architect and designer, and the Glasgow School of Painters again began to look forward. But when all is said and done, Victorian Scotland was the nursery of scientists rather than of artists, and of men of action rather than philosophers.

As the nineteenth century progressed, the increased importance of coal for heavy industry led to an even greater concentration of population in the central belt near to the mines. The demand for iron and steel, for ships and machinery, provided employment and a further (if still uneven) rise in living standards. But in the long run it rendered Scotland vulnerable when, first, foreign competition and, then, a slump severely curtailed markets. Scotland felt sorely the lack of diversification in her industry.

[2] Buried at Cults, Fife.
[3] Monument at Laurieston, Kirkcudbright.
[4] Illustration 94.

87. William Gladstone. This statue by Pittendrigh MacGillivray was moved from St Andrew Square, Edinburgh, to Coates Crescent, for which it had originally been intended, in 1955. The figure of the statesman in the appropriate robe of the Chancellor of the Exchequer is true to life; not so those of the Virtues who attend him—and distract attention from him. They are, however, adequately wrapped up against the Edinburgh winds, unlike two small boys who hold aloft a Greek inscription. Another statue of him stands in George Square, Glasgow.

Nor were her problems seen at first hand by her leading politicians. When faltering steps were taken towards a welfare state by the early Factory Acts, these were passed in London; and, in any case, the number of inspectors appointed to enforce the law was derisively small. Although such legislation more often than not was initiated by the Tories, the Scottish have-nots regarded the Whigs as a more likely source of remedies and, since many of the great landowners such as the Dukes of Argyll also supported that party (until Gladstone split it over Home Rule for Ireland), it reigned supreme so far

88. *The Rosebery Gallery, Dalmeny Church, West Lothian, renovated this century.*

as Scottish seats were concerned. But that was not enough to secure relief for Scottish grievances even when there was a Scottish and Liberal Prime Minister, because Gladstone spent far more time at Hawarden than he did at Fasque and, in the last resort, he was more concerned with Irish Land troubles than with Scottish ones. Furthermore as a High Anglican he had little sympathy with the Kirk. Nevertheless, if his United Kingdom achievements and his ideals for Home Rule be looked at as a whole (frustrated though they were), he may reasonably claim to have been the greatest of Scottish Prime Ministers.

The Earls of Aberdeen and of Rosebery were also Prime Minister and the latter is commemorated by the restoration of the family gallery in Dalmeny Church. Its woodwork is plain but the setting in the lovely Norman church is outstanding. The Prime Minister's son, the sixth Earl, erected it in memory of his father and also of his own eldest son, a gifted and much loved young man who if he had lived would surely have won distinction in some field, very likely that of politics.

A rival to Gladstone might be urged in Campbell-Banner-man.[5] He certainly held his party together as Prime Minister as no one expected that he would be able to do, and his stand during the Boer War set the new South Africa off on a hopeful course, and the Ministry over which he presided was the greatest reforming ministry until Attlee's. But he was given all too little time before his death, and the reforms which most benefited Scotland were those of Asquith and Lloyd George. And, by the time that Campbell-Bannerman achieved power, Scottish radicals were looking to a new party. Keir Hardie[6] had first stood as the Liberal candidate for North Ayrshire, but when he was unsuccessful, he founded the Scottish Labour Party in 1888. Its rise belongs to the next chapter.

A radical movement in the Highlands also produced a short-lived Crofters Party, which for a few years had a handful of M.P.s. The worst Clearances were over by then but crofters still had no security of tenure and no protection against the raising of rents. Most of their holdings were too small to support those who lived on them, and such a living as they could get from them was heavily dependent on their tradi-tional rights of grazing on the higher ground. When violence had extracted an Irish Land Act from the Parliament at West-minster it was not unnatural that similar legislation should be demanded for Scotland. The same year as the 1881 Act was passed for Ireland there was a failure of the vitally important potato crop and a poor return from the herring fishing on which many crofters relied to supplement their otherwise in-adequate returns. When in a time of sudden panic amongst lairds a naval gun boat was asked for to assist a plan to evict three crofters from Glendale in Skye, the tenants of another Skye laird decided to force the issue. The crofters of Braes, just

5 Buried at Meigle, Perthshire.
6 There are busts of Hardie at his home town, Cumnock, and in the Scottish National Portrait Gallery, and in the Houses of Parliament at Westminster.

89. *Memorial at Braes, Skye. In this lovely setting, a small stone pedestal bears a brass plate on which is engraved, first in Gaelic and then in English: "Near this cairn on the 19th of April 1882 ended the Battle fought by the people of the Braes on behalf of the crofters of Gaeldom." Equally remarkable in its setting but very different in size and in the man whom it commemorates is the huge statue of the first Duke of Sutherland by Chantrey on Beinn a Bhragaidh above Golspie.*

south of Portree, had always depended on grazing their cattle in summer on the slopes of Ben Lee but in the mid-nineteenth century Lord MacDonald had withdrawn leave and rented the pasture out to an incoming sheep farmer. In 1881 the latter's lease was due to run out and the crofters combined to offer a higher rent than the sitting tenant was paying, but this was refused. They then simply drove their beasts on to the slopes which, from time immemorial, had been common grazing. And, when a sheriff's officer arrived to serve an eviction order, the women of the township burnt the paper.

176

Retaliation on a grand scale was determined on, to serve as an example, to others. Fifty policemen, borrowed from Glasgow, with the sheriff leading them from behind, managed to arrest five of the ringleaders of the resistance; but getting them back to Portree was not so easy. It was necessary to pass through a defile where the only track lay between a precipitous cliff, going straight down to the sea, and a hillside almost as steep which provided an ideal vantage point from which the women showered boulders down on the police, all the while "howling in the most frightful manner". Fortunately no-one was killed. Equally fortunately, the courts took note of the depth of feeling which had been aroused. Two of the five men were fined fifty shillings and the other three twenty shillings each—and the fines were quickly paid on their behalf.

In fact the struggle was not quite over and another attempt was made later in the year, when most of the young men were away at the fishing, to enforce submission, but public opinion had been aroused. Lord MacDonald gave way and Gladstone's government was at last forced to realize that there was a Scottish as well as an Irish Land Problem. A Royal Commission was appointed under Lord Napier to look into "the condition of the crofters and cottars in the Highlands and Islands". For once a Royal Commission was followed by prompt action. Not all the problems were faced but by the Crofters Act of 1886, the crofter, for the first time, received security of tenure. He could no longer be evicted at will from house and livelihood and, with the coming of the Crofters Commission the next year, his rent could no longer be raised at will.

If the nineteenth century was an age of politics, it was no less an age in which men took an absorbing interest in religion, so much so that the Sabbatarianism, which proved so trying for the young, did not seem so to church-going adults; they went not only to listen to the sermon and to criticize it, but to enjoy it. Preaching provided the popular entertainment of the day, taking the place of newspaper, cinema, radio and television. Daily family prayer was widely used, religious issues were

90. The statue of Thomas Chalmers in George Street, Edinburgh, by Steell. One of the most remarkable men of the century, he was equally successful as a teacher of mathematics and chemistry when he was a young minister at Kilmany (his classes were greatly preferred to those of the professors at St Andrews), as a parish minister in the poorer parts of Glasgow and as Convener of the Church Expansion Committee (of the Established Church) when he raised £300,000 and built 220 new churches. And after the Disruption, he, more than anyone, was responsible for the swift success of the Free Church. But, above all, he was a man. "Never," it has been said, "did Scotland produce a greater or more lovable soul."

91. The statue of David Livingstone, Princes Street, Edinburgh, by Mrs D. O. Hill. David Livingstone was born in 1813 in Blantyre, where the tenement in which his parents lived has been preserved as an example of the housing of the time and to serve as a museum to illustrate his work. He entered a cotton factory at the age of ten but managed to educate himself so that by twenty-seven he was a qualified doctor and missionary. His greatest work was in exploring the Zambesi and much else of Central Africa and in arousing the conscience of the civilized world to the horrors of the Arab slave traffic. Another statue of him stands near the cathedral in Glasgow.

178

passionately argued, and parties were prepared to suffer if needs be for the sake of their opinions. In the eighteenth century, the seceders had been comparatively few in numbers and in influence. But when Thomas Chalmers withdrew in 1843 from the General Assembly of the Church of Scotland over the right of lairds to present ministers to "their" parishes and over the right of secular courts to rule on church matters, he was followed by well over a third of the ministers even though they knew that by so doing they were making themselves and their families homeless and forfeiting their means of livelihood. He has a statue in George Street, Edinburgh, and one of the most unusual of memorials—a lighthouse—in his birthplace, Anstruther, Fife.[7]

In fact, their action attracted much backing, and within ten years the Free Church had built 700 new churches and as many schools. No less deeply religious and no less ready to put behind them worldly things were the missionaries, male and female, for whom David Livingstone can stand representative.

Other missionaries from Scotland followed him in Africa, and other explorers. In Australia, John MacDouall Stuart from Dysart was the first to cross the continent from south to north in 1860 and Alexander Mackenzie explored the far north of Canada and crossed the Rockies to the Pacific coast.

This was an Imperial age in other ways, too. New Zealand's Dunedin took its name from Edinburgh and, in India, Colin Campbell, Lord Clyde, won distinction as a soldier, and the Marquis of Dalhousie as a statesman. Between 1847 when, at 35, he became the youngest ever Governor General and 1856, there was astonishing progress in the building of roads and railways, in the development of the Indian Civil Service, of trade, of agriculture and forestry, and in the suppression of suttee and thuggee. In Canada too, Scots were prominent in the political sphere and in developing communications. John MacDonald, the first Premier of the Dominion, had been born

---

[7] Another lighthouse memorial is that at Port Ellen, Islay, Argyll.

in Glasgow and Lord Strathcona (of the Canadian Pacific Railway) in Forres.

If it was an Imperial age, it was also a Royal age. For the first time for over two hundred years a sovereign was to make a home in Scotland and to feel affection for a country that had seemed an unmitigated nuisance to her German ancestors. She thought Edinburgh "quite beautiful, totally unlike anything else I have seen . . . and the people very friendly and kind", and she paid regular visits to Glasgow, Aberdeen and Dundee. She wrote enthusiastically about Staffa and Loch Maree and Glenfinnan, but it was the Highlands of Perthshire and Aberdeenshire that she knew best, travelling over rough roads and tracks, equally happily in a carriage, on horseback or on foot, indefatigable and always ready to ignore the weather except in so far as it obscured the view. Balmoral was to her the nearest approach to a home that she could enjoy, and it enabled her, she felt, to have human relationships and real conversation with ordinary people. And, though she was never in fact unaccompanied, she felt that she had a privacy there that nowhere else could give her. "This solitude, the romance and the wild loveliness of everything here . . . make Scotland the proudest, finest country in the world," she wrote, and each year she felt more and more the ending of her autumn holiday.

Wednesday, Sept 14 (1842)
This is our last day in Scotland; it really is a delightful country and I am sorry to leave it.

September 18, 1858
Alas! the last day! When we got up the weather seemed very hopeless. Everything was white with snow, which lay, at least, an inch on the ground, and it continued snowing heavily, as it had done since five this morning. I wished we might be snowed up, and unable to move. How happy I should have been could it have been so.

92. *Prince Albert was as devoted to Scotland as was the Queen, and Balmoral was very much his creation. This statue of Albert as the Queen liked to remember him, ready for the kill, was carved in white marble by William Theed the younger. It stands in the Queen's home and is therefore not visible to the public, but a bronze replica was presented to the tenants on the Balmoral estate and was placed near one of the entrances by which visitors are admitted to the gardens when members of the Royal Family are not in residence. Edinburgh, Glasgow and Aberdeen also have statues, and Dundee a splendid museum and art gallery in its appropriately Gothic Albert Institute. The best statue of the Queen herself is the massive one surmounting the National Gallery.*

The nineteenth century saw a scientific as well as an Industrial Revolution in which two Scots were pre-eminent, Clerk Maxwell and Kelvin. The former was descended from the Clerks of Penicuik, born and brought up in Edinburgh. He held the post of Professor of Natural Philosophy at Aberdeen University before going south to London and then on to Cambridge where at the Cavendish Laboratory he laid the foundations that were later to be built on by J. J. Thomson (a Manchester Scot) and Lord Rutherford, who came from New Zealand via a university in Montreal that had been founded by another Glaswegian, James McGill. Kelvin[8] came to Glasgow at the age of eight and lived there till his death after fifty-six years of teaching in its university; he was equally distinguished in pure and in applied science. Among the doctors were Joseph Lister, pioneer of antisepsis, and James Simpson, a baker's son, who entered the University in his own words "very young, very poor, very solitary and almost friendless", and earned the money to pay his fees by delivering morning rolls for his brother who had succeeded to the family shop. On the whole, science and religion were not yet in conflict, but there were some who objected to his use of chloroform in childbirth on the grounds that God had said of Woman: "In sorrow shalt thou bring forth children", to which Simpson's answer was: "I know. But I have also read that before God took a rib out of Adam's side, he cast him into a deep sleep." There is a statue of him in Princes Street and a plaque on the door of his house, 52 Queen Street, Edinburgh, where he first experimented on himself; and the Maternity Pavilion at the Royal Infirmary is named after him. Towards the end of the century, Colonel David Bruce and Major Ronald Ross did much to prevent tropical disease by their discovery of the part played by the tse-tse fly and the mosquito in spreading fever and malaria.

Last but not least in the services he rendered through his benefactions, is Andrew Carnegie. The son of an impoverished hand-loom weaver from Dunfermline, he was taken to

---

[8] Statue in Kelvinside Park, Glasgow.

America at the age of thirteen. A man of steel, he made a fortune in steel and ploughed £70,000,000 of it back into various forms of education including countless free libraries, swimming-baths and playing-fields before local authorities entered that field, and £10,000,000 to the Scottish universities. His early home has been preserved but his finest memorial is the Pittencrieff Park from which as a child he had been barred but which he eventually managed to buy for his home town.

93. *The Bannockburn Memorial, Stirling. Bruce's statue in bronze by C.d'O. Pilkington Jackson was unveiled by Her Majesty the Queen in 1964. The site of the battle over which it looks is now largely built up, but the National Trust for Scotland has provided an audio-visual presentation illustrating the background to the Wars of Independence.*

TEN

The Latest Age

The twentieth no less than the nineteenth century saw new developments. The statue on its pedestal, solemn and too often uninspired, is gradually superseded by a much wider variety of memorial, and by a much more imaginative treatment. The bas-relief of R. L. Stevenson by A. St Gaudens is so strikingly different in style from the marble and heraldic monuments to Montrose and Argyll, that it may serve as a bridge between the old and the new.

A man's birthplace may well be much more revealing than a statue and the National Trust for Scotland has done well to preserve those of Andrew Carnegie, David Livingstone, Hugh Miller and James Barrie, all men of humble origins whose cottages illustrate a way of life now past.

Gardens too have been created as memorials, as for instance at Coldstream overlooking the Tweed to mark the raising by Monck of that regiment;[1] at Kirkcaldy near the station for a War Memorial; and in Perth, by the Tay, in memory of Sir Stanley Norie-Miller who, with his father, did so much to keep Scottish insurance business in Scotland and to attract it from further afield.

Even when a statue has remained central to a monument,

---

[1] In fact, the regiment was not raised there; it had been in existence for ten years before it entered the Royal service and marched from there to England to proclaim the Restoration of Charles II.

94. *Robert Louis Stevenson in St Giles, Edinburgh.* The son and grandson of lighthouse engineers, he turned, through ill health, to literature and proved equally successful as a writer of essays, stories of adventure for young and old, and tales as different as Dr Jekyll and Mr Hyde and Weir of Hermiston. *He died in Samoa in 1894. He is also commemorated in Edinburgh in the house in Howard Place where he was born, which contains relics associated with his life and work. James Stewart of the Glens, who features in his* Kidnapped, *is remembered near the place of his hanging at Ballachulish after the Appin Murder of 1752.*

95. *Barrie, 1860–1937, was the son of a strongly religious handloom weaver and of Margaret Ogilvie, who had an even deeper influence on him. Having gone to England to earn his living as a journalist, he first made his name by recreating scenes from the Kirriemuir life of his parents' days—* Auld Licht Idylls *and* A Window in Thrums—*but after a novel* The Little Minister *had been successfully dramatized, he turned almost entirely to play-writing. The contents of his birthplace include manuscripts, letters and two of the hair-bottomed chairs that his father bought for the house on the day that James was born, so that the ground-floor which had been his workshop could be converted into a parlour. Outside is still the communal wash-house where, as a child, he staged and acted his first play and which gave him the idea for the Wendy House in* Peter Pan.

more thought has been paid to its setting. No one could wish for a more superb site for a monument than that near Stirling for the Wallace Monument but the tower is grim; it is best seen at a distance, as indeed it can be for miles round, than as a background to the figure of the Guardian of the Realm. A hundred years later the National Trust for Scotland has provided a rotunda in which a vigorous equestrian statue of Robert I can be better appreciated.

Lack of money has of course been one factor in the neglect of the full-length statue but this has not always been a disadvantage. There are some excellent busts in the National Portrait Gallery in Queen Street, Edinburgh in which the subject's character can be better appreciated than on a lofty pedestal, notably those by Epstein and by Schotz.

Quite different—and inspired—was the conception of the Queen Victoria School at Dunblane for the sons of Scots serving in the armed forces. It was a memorial jointly to the Queen and to those killed in the South African War. In the same tradition, the Cameron Highlanders founded a Boys Club in Inverness after the Second World War.

Different yet again are memorials, not to an individual nor to a specific event, but to a bygone age, a former style of living, as for example the Georgian House in Edinburgh, and Gladstone's Land, and the agrarian and folk museums at Auchendrain and Pitmedden, Ceres, Glamis and Kingussie. Indeed it has been suggested that the decline of statuary may have been due less to economic stringency or a dearth of outstanding men and women than to the standardization and depersonalization of life at all levels, as well as to the growing tendency of art to become abstract.

Naturally the opening few years of the century are the most traditional. The South African War was still going on, and most Scottish regiments have their memorials to those who were killed. And Edward VII has representations of his portly figure in the greater cities, but he was the last sovereign to be so honoured. In general, there was more enthusiasm for the physical courage of the soldiers than for the moral courage of the

Liberal Leader, Campbell-Bannerman, who had protested against the concentration camps with a phrase that became famous—"methods of barbarism". It probably contributed to his loss of the Khaki Election which followed immediately on the peace but he did not have to wait long for his revenge on Balfour, and in 1906 won a truly landslide victory, the last blaze of Liberal glory. Though he himself was to die all too soon, it was his success that enabled Asquith[2] to introduce Old Age Pensions and National Health Insurance and to curb the powers of the House of Lords. John Burns became the first Cabinet Minister who had worked with his hands (as an engineering apprentice); and, supporting these measures was the first Labour Member of Parliament, a miner, James Keir Hardie. Scotland gained greatly and she nearly gained more, in spite of the fact that Ireland was still the Liberals' prime concern. Since Ireland was to have Home Rule, there was also a Home Rule Bill for Scotland on the stocks when war broke out in 1914.

Some 200,000 Scots who died in the First World War are commemorated in a National War Memorial in Edinburgh Castle that has justly become famous, and they, and others, in the Scottish United Services Museum there.

A number of Scots reached high command, including Sir Ian Hamilton who directed the Dardanelles Campaign, and Earl Haig who succeeded Sir John French in command of all the British troops on the Western Front in 1915. Haig's generalship has been argued over but no-one has ever questioned his courage or his determination, nor the way in which he worked, after the War, for all ex-soldiers. He is the only person individually honoured in the National War Memorial; he has an equestrian statue on the Edinburgh Castle Esplanade and one in London; and he could of course have been buried in St Paul's or Westminster Abbey. But he preferred his own Border country (a grateful nation had

[2] A Yorkshireman but a Scottish M.P.—for East Fife from 1886–1918 and for Paisley from 1920–4.

96. *The National War Memorial, Edinburgh Castle. The overall design is by Sir Robert Lorimer, who also chose the individual craftsmen; it has great dignity and attempts something new; it remembers not just the famous generals; all ranks are given equal representation, as are also the supporting services in the field and those at home who worked in the factories and on the land and beneath it. Even the pack animals are remembered, even the mice and the canaries, the Tunnellers' friends. In the illustration, the central shrine may be seen with its green Stone of Remembrance which rests on the bare rock which has been allowed to rise above the floor. Behind it, a bronze frieze by Alice and Morris Meredith-Williams shows some sixty separate figures, each in his or her working or battle dress. The same humble and earthy treatment is*

190

97. *Much lovely masonry survives at Dryburgh Abbey, founded in 1150 by monks from Alnwick. Scott lies in St Mary's Aisle. Haig's simple head-stone though carved by C. d'O. Pilkington Jackson, is of the same pattern as those of countless of his comrades in arms who lie in War Cemeteries throughout the world. Among a number of other interesting memorials in the precincts, the Buchan Pillar was erected by the eleventh Earl of Buchan* to his forebears in 1794. It is of red sandstone, about ten feet high and still in good condition. On three of its sides it bears representations in low relief of James I, James II and Hugo de Norvil, King's Banneret. Not far away is another tribute by the same Earl—a colossal statue with legs like oak trees (and the rest to match) to: "WALLACE Great Patriot Hero Ill requited Chief A.D.MDCCCXIV Joannes Smith sculpsit."*

* The Earl was the moving spirit in the founding of the Society of Antiquaries of Scotland. He died at Dryburgh in 1829 and is buried there.

DOUGLAS HAIG

BORN IN EDINBURGH JUNE 19TH 1861 : DEPARTED OUT OF THIS WORLD SUNDAY JAN. 29TH 1928

HE TRUSTED IN GOD AND TRIED TO DO THE RIGHT

evident in the pictures in the lightly tinted stained glass of Douglas Strachan in the main Hall of Honour where each Service and each Regiment has its own bay. There is only one individual honoured, Earl Haig. Much else is worthy of study, especially in the carving of the stone, both inside and on the exterior of the building. Among the contributing sculptors were C. d'O. Pilkington Jackson, Phyllis Bone, Alexander Carrick and J. H. Clark.

After the Second World War, it was decided not to make any alterations which might detract from the unity of the original conception, but simply to add further names to the Rolls of Honour.

Ian Hay's book about the Memorial has long been out of print, but a short guide, obtainable in the Castle, has some excellent illustrations and much information about the details and the artists, and explains the difficulties involved in placing, on that critical and vulnerable site, a building which would harmonize with its surroundings.

restored Bemersyde to the Haigs) and lies near Scott in Dryburgh Abbey.

A world-wide war on such a scale as that of 1914–18 was totally different from anything that had been seen before, and it shaped Scotland's future. Though it produced a temporary halt in the decline of heavy industry by calling for ever more ships and guns, and did much the same for agriculture when the submarine blockade required that land should be cultivated which could never in the long run yield an economic return, the end results were disastrous. And, when peace came, there was no prepared plan for readjustment. The Highland areas were increasingly depopulated and there was widespread unemployment throughout the industrial central belt; and, even for those who managed to keep their jobs, wages did not keep pace with inflation. All this led to support for those Labour leaders who had already been protesting against such things as the dilution of labour in the war factories, and the calls which had been made on them to give up so many of the hard-won achievements of the Trade Union movement. For twenty years between the wars, Scottish M.P.s were a force on the left wing of the Labour Party. Known as the Clydesiders (though they did not all represent constituencies from that region) men such as Maxton, Kirkwood, Wheatley and Shinwell made their mark and in the 1922 election, though the Tories won an overall victory by 347 to Labour's 142 and the Liberals' 117, the Scottish electors returned 29 Labour M.P.s to the Tories' 15 and the Liberals' 17. It was Maxton who caught the eye with his distinguished appearance and fiery speeches, but, in the long run, it was Tom Johnston who was to achieve most—and that not until the Second World War. Wheatley's contribution was the 1924 Housing Act; Kirkwood's the agitation which eventually led to the restarting of work on the *Queen Mary* which had been abandoned during the slump of the Thirties. Shinwell is happily still with us and it is too early to assess his work at the Ministries of Mines and of Defence. Never in Parliament, but a father figure, was the Communist John Maclean, to whom a cairn has recently been

98. *The memorial to Ramsay MacDonald overlooking his birthplace, Lossiemouth. MacDonald (1866–1937) joined the Independent Labour Party in 1893, became its Secretary in 1900 and M.P. 1906. He was Prime Minister January–November 1924 and 1929–31, in which year he resigned and formed a National Government. On the first occasion he lost the support of the Left and fumbled over the Zinovier letter; on the second he failed to carry more than a handful of his Labour supporters with him. His best work was done in his early years, and he showed considerable courage in opposing the First World War and as Foreign Secretary, a post which he held with that of Prime Minister in 1924.*

erected in Pollokshaws, Glasgow, which proclaims that "he forged the Scottish link in the golden chain of world socialism". Within Parliament, the two extremes are often thought of as Maxton and Ramsay MacDonald[3] but the antithesis is false, and it was in fact the influence of Maxton that originally made MacDonald leader of the Labour Party, and therefore, in due course, Prime Minister. It was only the

---

[3] Both have busts that are worthy of them. Maxton by Benno Schotz is in the Kelvingrove Art Gallery, Glasgow; MacDonald by Epstein is in the National Portrait Gallery, Edinburgh.

cumulative pressures of office, of the General Strike (of which he disapproved), and the financial crises arising from the slump of 1929–31, together with age and ill-health, that modified MacDonald's outlook.

In the Second World War, as in the First, Scottish regiments earned the gratitude of their fellow countrymen and the awed respect of their opponents all over the world, but once again the drain on manpower was disastrous—and on the economy equally so. Of the leaders, Admiral Cunningham after commanding the Mediterranean Fleet played an even more vital part as a member of the Chiefs of Staff, and his brother commanded with great success in East Africa before being replaced in the Western Desert by first Ritchie and then Auchinleck—and some people would claim that his judgement was no more at fault than theirs, and that, without adequate armour and air support, his troops could do no more. Two other outstanding generals had earlier served with Scottish regiments, Field Marshal Earl Wavell (there are gates to his honour at the Black Watch Headquarters in Perth) and General Sir Richard O'Connor.

If Scott Sutherland has, in Illustration 99, typified the ruggedness of war, another living sculptor has captured (in Illustrations 100 and 101) very surely the lovingness of motherhood and the long thoughts of boyhood.

The year 1945 saw for the first time a Labour Government in power with a sufficient majority to carry through its policies but these did not always work to Scottish advantage; indeed, as one M.P. gibed, "too often Nationalization meant for Scotland Denationalization" as control of the nationalized industries became centred in London. Furthermore, Tom Johnston who had been such a success as Secretary of State for Scotland in the wartime Coalition Government, not least for

99. The memorial to the Commandos, Spean Bridge, 1952. It was in this part of Scotland that the Commandos did much of their training. Scott Sutherland, the sculptor of this resolute group, also designed the Black Watch Memorial in Dundee and the Leaping Salmon fountain for the Norie-Miller Memorial Garden in Perth.

UNITED WE CONQUER

IN·MEMORY·OF
THE·OFFICERS·AND
MEN·OF
THE·COMMANDOS
WHO·DIED·IN·THE
SECOND·WORLD·WAR
1939-1945
THIS·COUNTRY·WAS
THEIR·TRAINING
GROUND

his creation of the North of Scotland Electricity Board (with all that that meant for the remoter areas), retired from politics and, apart from Lord Shinwell, one searches in vain for Scots among the more prominent Labour politicians—Attlee, Bevin, Bevan, Morrison, Wilson, Callaghan, Foot, Healey, Benn. The old Liberal tradition has been kept alive by Grimond and Steel but their supporters are as yet too few to allow them any considerable influence. Of the Tories, Harold Macmillan was of Highland extraction but, as a London publisher who represented an English constituency, he lived and worked in the south—and the most outstanding achievements of Lord Home of the Hirsel were in Foreign rather than in domestic affairs.

It is hardly surprising, in the circumstances, that there was an upsurge in Scottish Nationalism. Without proportional representation it made little headway in electoral terms until the Seventies when the dubious slogan "It's Scotland's Oil" gave the Party their highest total of eleven M.P.s in a Parliament in which a Labour Government had no overall majority. Under pressure a Devolution Act was passed with a condition that it should not be brought into effect unless a Referendum of voters registered in Scotland should show 40% of those voting to be in favour. A majority of those voting were in favour, but not 40%—and there the matter rests. The Conservatives, who came into power shortly after the Referendum, had said that they were not opposed to Devolution in principle, only to the Bill actually laid before Parliament, but they have as yet shown no anxiety to come up with a scheme of their own.

Alongside this political nationalism is a resurgence of interest in the Gaelic tongue and Gaelic singing and music and, in the Lowlands, the Lallans movement. For Barrie and for Buchan ambition had meant residence in England. So too, journalism had called Leslie Mitchell south but his imaginative writing (under the *nom de plume* of Lewis Grassic Gibbon) remained essentially Scottish; and, at home, Hugh Mac-Diarmid (C. M. Grieve) spearheaded a Renaissance which

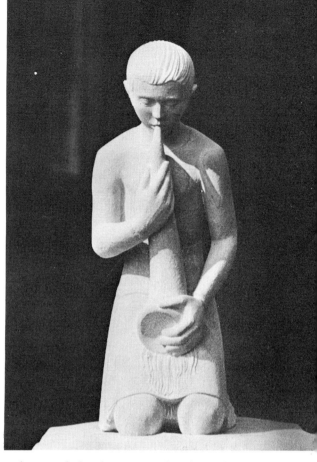

100. The figure of a shepherd boy for a West Highland graveyard, by Hew Lorimer.

thrives in both prose and verse, helped, as music has been, by radio and television. His memorial is to be a Chair of Scottish Literature in one of our universities.

In the development of these, three Scots—also exiles for most of their working lives—played vital, if differing parts: John Reith, the first director of the B.B.C.,[4] J. Logie Baird, pioneer of television, and Sir R. Watson Watt who did so much to develop radar. For other scientists, some of them still living, Alexander Fleming may stand representative. Having left his country school at thirteen, the only secondary schooling he got was two years at a polytechnic. Then at sixteen he took a job as a clerk in London, to earn the money to pay for a

---

[4] Commemorated by the B.B.C.'s Reith Lectures.

101. *The statue of Our Lady of the Isles, South Uist. Hew Lorimer, the sculptor, is the son of Sir Robert Lorimer, the architect of the National War Memorial. The twenty-seven-foot-high column of Creetown granite is, in its way, a memorial to the faithfulness of those Catholics in some of the islands and remote parts of the West Highlands who never yielded to the Reformers despite considerable harassment.*

medical training, rising at five o'clock each morning to fill the considerable gaps in his knowledge. Such a background might well have been an excellent preparation for life as a research worker but equally it might have turned him into an introvert, never taking his mind off his particular scientific quest. In fact, his boyhood made him a fully rounded person. "We had many advantages over boys living in towns," he said later, "we got many of the things they missed, climbing, guddling trout, sheep and shepherding", and he valued the long walks to school because they gave him time to think. So, as a man, he swam and played water polo and shot at Bisley, and gardened and fished. And, at the end, at St Mary's Hospital in London, his quest was successful and he discovered the healing properties of penicillin. His tomb in St Paul's is of marble from Greece, and, apart from his initials, bears only a lily for St Mary's and a Thistle for Scotland; they were the three places which meant most to him.

Finally, even if the main day of the week in Scotland is now Saturday and not Sunday, and if the main subject of disputation is now football rather than the sermon, no account of the twentieth century would be complete without reference to the healing in 1929 of the breach between the Established Church and most of the Free Church movement, nor the growing, if as yet unrealized, efforts to achieve an even wider ecumenical reunion; harmony has at least been reached among leaders of all denominations, and there is undreamed of co-operation at grass roots in many places. It was as an ecumenical gesture that in 1906 the eighth Duke of Argyll gave the Abbey of Iona to the Church of Scotland for the use of all men. Restored by the Iona Community, its very future seemed recently at risk when news came that the remainder of the island was up for sale, but it was bought for over a million pounds to be a memorial to Lord Fraser of Allandale. What finer memorial could a man have? What better ending for a book on the memorials of Scotland?

APPENDIX

Monuments of Edinburgh

Edinburgh has the greatest concentration of monuments and they are too numerous to list in full. However, we are shortly promised the Edinburgh volume of *The Buildings of Scotland* by David Walker, to be published by Penguin in conjunction with the National Trust for Scotland.

Certain areas are specially prolific. The Castle has military memorials on the Esplanade, including Earl Haig. Either side of the gateway are modern statues to Wallace (by Carrick) and Bruce (by Clapperton). Within is St Margaret's Chapel and the National War Memorial (Illustrations 16 and 96).

In the Royal Mile, Knox, Charles II (Illustration 63) and the fifth Duke of Buccleuch stand outside St Giles, and memorials to Moray, Montrose, Argyll (Illustration 61) and R. L. Stevenson (Illustration 94) are inside. Opposite is Parliament Hall (Illustration 71) which makes a magnificent setting for the legal history of Scotland; Scott is there by Greenshields and Cockburn by Brodie, but the two most interesting are by Chantrey—the first Viscount Melville, massive and imposing, and his nephew, Robert Dundas, arrestingly thoughtful. The most famous is Roubiliac's Duncan Forbes of Culloden. Further down, in the Canongate Churchyard, Adam Smith is buried and many other distinguished Scots including Robert Fergusson, over whom Burns raised a simple stone, and, reputedly, Rizzio. From it there is a good view of the Grecian Burns Monument by Hamilton, standing below the former

Royal High School. Outside Holyrood a statue and elaborate iron gates commemorate Edward VII, and, in the ruins of the Abbey, there are wall tablets to Adam Bothwell, Bishop of Orkney who died in 1593, Alexander Hay who died in 1594 and the Countess of Eglinton who died in 1596.

Outside Robert Adam's Register House is Wellington by Steell (Illustration 76). Then, on the south side of Princes Street—reading from east to west—come Livingstone (1875 by Mrs Amelia Hill, Illustration 91) and Scott (Illustration 84); the former Lord Provost Adam Black (1877 by Hutchinson), "Christopher North" (Professor John Wilson) by Steell, Alan Ramsay the poet (Steell), the Scots Greys Boer War Memorial, Rev. Thomas Guthrie (F. W. Pomeroy), a friendly statue to Simpson the pioneer of the use of chloroform, and a pseudo-Celtic cross to Dean Ramsay, minister of the nearby Episcopal Church of St John and author of *Reminiscences of Scottish Life and Character*. Within the gardens are a statue entitled "The Call 1914" (a tribute from an American sculptor R. Tait MacKenzie) and an unshaped rock, placed there to commemorate the joint resolve of Norwegians and Scots against Nazi aggression from 1939–45. At the eastern end, a semi-circular arcade designed by Sir Frank Mears provides the backcloth for bronze work by C.d'O. Pilkington Jackson, and stone carving by a number of sculptors—the regimental memorial of the Royal Scots.

In George Street, there is a vista of statues from Charlotte Square to St Andrew Square. In the former, there is the Prince Consort (the most peace-loving of men) in the uniform of a Field Marshal, with, on his plinth, bas reliefs of episodes in his life and quotations from his speeches, and—less happily—groups of mourners at each corner. Then come the Rev. Thomas Chalmers (Steell, Illustration 90), Pitt and George IV (Chantrey), the first Viscount Melville on his column (Illustration 83), and finally the soldier fourth Earl of Hopetoun by Thomas Campbell.

Queen Street has the Gothic Revival building which houses the National Museum of Antiquities and the National Portrait

Gallery of Scotland; its exterior carries figures of most of Scotland's notables but they are not always easy to see, let alone identify, except on the front facing St Andrew Street where the light is better and Mary Stewart and her ladies can be appreciated. Inside are some splendid heads—R. Cunninghame Graham, Hugh MacDiarmid and J. Ramsay MacDonald by Epstein; the sculptor Pittendrigh MacGillivray by Benno Schotz;[1] John Buchan, W. E. Henley, Thomas Carlyle, and Raeburn. There are also busts of William Adam and James Watt, and full-length statues of Burns and Carlyle. Unfortunately the head of Fleming reveals little of the greatness of the man.

Calton Hill has its own group of monuments (Illustration 80) and a finely landscaped cemetery below, a littler earlier than that of the Glasgow Necropolis; David Hume is buried here and there is a monument to the radicals who suffered in the political trials of the 1790s, whereas Greyfriars' Churchyard commemorates the Covenanters taken at Bothwell Brig in 1679 and imprisoned there; it is also particularly rich in seventeenth-century monuments, including that erected by George Heriot to his father.

[1] Benno Schotz, Queen's sculptor in ordinary for Scotland, also carved the busts of Keir Hardie for the Houses of Parliament at Westminster and at Cumnock.

Index

Bold type refers to illustrations

M
cl.